I love all these stories! They're so good! ☺

Love you sooooo much!

Leigh Annie

(also known as "I")

↗

little I, that is...

It kind of looks like eyelashes & a nose! hai" ☺

Living

in

Revival

IIII
O
↑
that turned out looking like a yelling person in need of a haircut... oops

The Everyday Lifestyle of the Normal Christian

David and Kathie Walters

Living in Revival

ISBN 978-1-888081-18-3

Printed in USA by Good News Ministries

Table of Contents

INTRODUCTION

It was a number of years after we came into a tremendous revival and wonderful body ministry that we began to see how Christianity had changed from when it started as a movement in the book of Acts and 300 years later ended up as a religion. So many things that we came into we knew in our hearts that this was really the norm for the church, but so many church-goers hadn't a clue. After reading *'1700 Years is Long Enough'* by James Rutz in 1990 and *'Pagan Christianity'* by George Barna and Frank Viola, years later, we realized that for the most part we had stayed on track, even though we were in a minority.

Christian religious hierarchy which has given us the clergy, large religious buildings, prestigious pulpits, famous orators, theological Bible colleges and Bible students, denominations, prophets, evangelists and missionaries; by and large has had a successful effect upon society in declaring that religion still has a major part to play in our day. It offers good alternatives to many negative and destructive forces that we face today and hopefully holds back the tide of godless secularism and the atheistic agenda. But it's only one side to the purpose of Christianity. The internal, spiritual life of walking and living in the supernatural and equipping every saint to fulfill their personal God given destiny is still lacking in many cases and in many churches.

What is the purpose of the average church going Joe or Jane? Is it to be faithful in attending Sunday morning worship with their tithes and offerings and listen to the pastor's monologue and stay out of trouble? Are their religious lives locked up in supporting a leader's vision and occasionally swoon under the anointed hands of their religious heroes or Christian superstars? Or is there more? Does God have a supernatural plan and adventures available for every believer? Surely He must have and in this book we hope to show you (the average Christian.) Your ordinary life can become extraordinary!

The house church movement which we were involved in the early seventies spread across England like wildfire. What God could do and was doing through ordinary people blew our minds. When we traveled to America more wonderful things happened at the house fellowships as well as churches in many States. Revelations, songs, healings, salvations and deliverance took place. When the extreme hierarchical *'Shepherding Movement'* reared its ugly head in the early seventies, by and large it thwarted the freedom of the Spirit in many churches and fellowships.

As a reaction against the 'Heavy Shepherding' movement a number of the fellowships believed and started to teach that 'equal eldership' was Biblical. When they met they wanted 100% agreement on decisions, so most of the time nothing was achieved. They made the mistake of replacing the Biblical concept of 'plural' eldership for the unbiblical concept of 'equal' eldership.

Although every believer is equal in the sight of God, (we are saved by grace.) not everyone is equal in the sight of God as far as abilities, gifts, anointing, or experience. The word "Elder' denotes an older mature person. Back in those days there were many youngsters in their twenties ordained as elders ministering in these free fellowships. A young apprentice Elder is not equal to a well seasoned, mature Elder. So eventually you will have a need for a presiding Elder who will need to make the final decisions if there is an impasse. As said, 'the buck stops here.' Also all Elders should have at least one of the five fold ministry gifts operating in their lives. (See Eph. 4: 11)

Some years after we moved to the U.S. we found that some of the large churches were breaking down into house groups, but for the most part it was nothing like we had experienced. They would have weekly house meetings overseen by an elder; usually the house owner and they would have a format. Generally it was to discuss the pastor's last Sunday's sermon. There wasn't any spontaneity or gifts of the spirit operating. The 'H-2-H' house church movement which I once spoke at their yearly convention was quite organized and didn't appear to be anymore free in the Spirit than the large church house meetings. In their house meetings the children were usually put in another room to play or watch a movie while the adults dealt with problems by sharing and having counseling. They felt it would be inappropriate for children to be there when couples were discussing subjects such as their marriage problems. I suggested that the children could comeback and participate in prayer and spiritual ministry at the completion of the counseling sessions. Community is good if it's based on spiritual principles and not on soulish or humanistic emotions. Jesus didn't sympathize with people; He delivered them. The Apostle Paul said, *"Therefore, from now on, we regard no one according to the flesh. Even though we have known Christ according to the flesh, yet now we know Him no longer."* (2.Cor. 5:16)

It's the 'life' first, then the New Testament pattern. The early church taught out of their supernatural experience. Today, many try to have the teaching first, but then lack the supernatural. It's like putting the cart before the horse. We found that when people came to us with serious problems they were usually delivered in the meetings, because of the strong presence of the Holy Spirit.

In the early church the disciples were told to heal the sick and cast out demons, not to take a course and get a degree in Christian counseling; of course where the reality of God and the presence of the Holy Spirit is lacking, then the best we can offer is "Christian psychology.". . . . if there is such a biblical term?

We trust that the exciting, amazing accounts and stories in this book will stir you up to believe for God's best for His church. If it happened in the seventies, it can happen again today. Not necessary identical, but having the freedom of the spirit and living in the supernatural. Why settle for plan 'B' when God is still working His perfect plan. Enjoy and be challenged by the accounts in this book and remember 'good' can become the enemy of God. "Go for the gold." as they say.

David & Kathie Walters

7

Living in Revival

Chapter one
Becoming a Christian

I was raised a Catholic. My father was Jewish and my mother was Catholic, so she insisted that my older sister, my younger brother and I were to be baptized as Catholics, so during our childhood we all attended Mass. When my sister made her first communion; after the service they all went to the fellowship hall for a special breakfast. I told my Mom that I wanted some breakfast as well. She replied, "You can't! You haven't made your first communion." Immediately I responded with, "I want to make my first communion!" I just wanted to get to that breakfast. Later I became an altar boy, not because I was spiritual, but altar boys got to go to the circus and zoo for free. Like lots of kids today, I went to church for the wrong reason. When I didn't feel like going my mother told me I needed to keep my religion up.

During my teens I became friendly with a boy named Ralph at a local youth center. He played boogie on the piano and also table tennis. He was 21 and I was 15. We hung out together a lot and he taught me to play table tennis at which I excelled. We often played five evenings a week and sometimes we would practice for eight hours at a time on the weekends.

When I talked to him about religion he said he was an Agnostic. When I was 18 I enlisted for three years in the Air Force; which was mandatory to serve for at least two years in one of the three armed forces. I was sent to serve in Malta for the last fifteen months of my 3 year enlistment. It was during that time that I rebelled against the official Catholic teaching that taught that when the Pope was speaking on doctrine or morals, he was infallible. I just couldn't see it.

After returning from my tour of duty in 1955 and becoming demobilized I saw my friend again and we picked up where we left off. We hung out together for a few more years. He finally met a girl and got married and we lost touch for a while.

It was in 1959 that once again we renewed our friendship and he told me that he had become a Christian. He then started witnessing to me, but I kept saying, "I am a Christian because I was baptized a Catholic." He kept on about having a personal relationship with Jesus Christ and accepting Him into my life. I argued with him. Sometime later, he invited me over to his house and while we were talking, he phoned a friend named Timmy who was an actor. Timmy rode several miles on his bicycle just to witness to me. What impressed me was the fact that he was willing to ride all that way, because he was concerned about my soul. I thought, "Well maybe I should be concerned about my soul

9

as well." They invited me to attend their church the next Sunday morning. As I wasn't attending mass anymore I accepted. I traveled about 12 miles from my suburban area up to Buckingham Gate, London to a rather depressing looking 18th century building which was just around the corner from Buckingham Palace where the Queen lived.

This was the first time I had ever been inside a Protestant church which was much less ornate than a Catholic church. There were no pretty stained glass windows, or statues of Jesus, Mary, the Apostles or the Saints. It was a large oval shape building that had two balconies which went all the way round. The building seated about 1,500 to 2,000 people. Instead of an altar, there was a huge pulpit with a huge organ behind it which reached to the ceiling. We sat down in a pew on the main level to the left of the pulpit which was about twelve feet high. It was really more like a large circular rostrum. The morning service started at 11.00 am. A small man around sixty with a balding head surrounded by white hair and dressed in a black gown mounted the stairs of the rostrum. Unknown to me at the time this was the great Welsh expository preacher, Dr. Martyn Lloyd Jones. I was in Westminster Chapel. London.

Traditionally, the Sunday morning service was for teaching Christian doctrine. The Organ started with a praise song,

"*Praise God from all whom blessings flow,*
Praise Him all creatures here below,
Praise Him above the heavenly host,
Praise Father Son and Holy Ghost, Amen!"

This was sung in rather a solemn way. I preferred the nicer tunes that we had in the Catholic Church, especially the hymns to Mary. This was my first experienced of what was known as the 'hymn sandwich.' Which is an opening hymn, a long prayer, another hymn, the reading of the word, another hymn, the notices and the offering, the preaching of the word (which lasted for about 50 minutes, which I wasn't used to) the closing hymn and finally the benediction. The service lasted about 90 minutes. The only thing I remember about that sermon was that the preacher kept saying 'therefore' and 'wherefore' and I was trying to figure out the difference. On reflection, the reading, the sermon, and the hymns, were in Elizabethan English. Being uneducated in any kind of doctrine or preaching, I was obviously very ignorant.

Ralph then invited me back for lunch at this large three story town house in Kensington which was owned by a commercial movie director called Derek and his wife Marion, who was a former model. They were both Christians. The house had a long comfortable lounge and several people were present eating and talking. It was known as the 'Antioch' as it was named after the place where the early disciples were first called Christians. Then Timmy, Ralph's actor friend, came and witnessed to me again. I remember it quite well when he was emphasizing committing my life to Christ.

After a lot of talking I told him to come and see me when I am about sixty, because I wanted to do my thing right now. He replied that there was no guarantee that I would be able to do that and the time to commit was now. He quoted, *"Boast not of thyself of tomorrow; for thou knowest not what a day may bring forth."* (Prov.27:1)

I then argued that I wouldn't be able to keep it up, but he said, that Christ would keep me up. After some more persuasion I said a prayer and made a commitment. Two weeks later my friend invited me back to Westminster Chapel for the Sunday evening 6.00 pm gospel service. Dr. Martyn Lloyd-Jones preached a powerful salvation message and everything fell into place. I was in a Calvinist Church so there were no altar calls as the *'Doctor'* as he was known as by the chapel members, didn't believe in altar calls as God was sovereign and didn't need man's help. He felt that if people responded emotionally through men's persuasion, then it wasn't of the Spirit.

After the service we went back to the movie director's house again. Timmy came over and spoke to me for a while then he introduced me to Derek, the director. After saying he was pleased that I had become a Christian he asked me what I was going to do about it.

I said, "I don't know."

So he replied, "Well, we will see you at church on Sunday morning."

I said, "That would be fine."

"And Sunday evening," he added.

I asked, "Sunday evening as well?"

He replied, "Do you have anything better to do on a Sunday evening?"

My habit had been to go to the coffee bar on Sunday afternoon to meet my friends and then go to the movies about 4.00 pm and then go dancing after the movie was over.

I obviously couldn't say, "Yes going dancing; looking for girls is more important." So I said, "No!"

Then he continued, "We have what we call the 'baby basket' for new Christians that we want you to attend every Thursday evening for six weeks. This will enable you to learn the basics and grow in your Christian life."

Then he gave me a little 'Navigator' booklet, *'Beginning, With Christ'* which had four scripture verses for me to learn. He also gave me a Bible and told me to read through John's Gospel.

I enjoyed attending the Thursday 'baby basket' as they had a different speaker each week, including Timmy and Derek and they were all very interesting in covering different subjects ranging from Christian apologetics, evangelism, prayer, Bible study, to church procedure. Halfway though the six weeks Derek told me to read through the four gospels and gave me eight more verses to learn from another 'Navigator' booklet called, *'Going On With Christ.'*

After the six weeks were completed, Derek introduced me to a young man.

"This is John and he will be taking care of you. He will be your follow-up. You will meet with him every Thursday evening and he will answer any questions, or any temptations you may encounter and help you to grow and mature in your Christian life."

Then he gave me a booklet with 120 scripture verses to learn and said, "Read the whole of the New Testament, (except for the Book of Revelation) attend church Sunday morning and evening, meet with John on Thursday evening, attend our by-weekly Tuesday evening prayer meeting and our bi-weekly Wednesday evening Bible study; and tithe 10% of your income to the work of the Lord; Any Questions?"

Being a former Catholic, I didn't know that most protestant churchgoers don't do what was required of me. So I was discipled and taught personal evangelism. I was very successful as I witnessed to everyone, especially my friends. If I was stuck (where I couldn't answer their questions) during witnessing to my potential fish, (as we called them) I would take them to see Timmy or Derek. As I watched the way they dealt with the arguments; I learned from them, as they were the experts and it was very seldom that the fish got away, once they had their hooks in them. After all, we were called to be 'fishers of men.' At this point I was not spirit-filled, as were all of us, so our evangelistic endeavors were much on the intellectual Christian apologetics level.

For the most part we tended to be known as the worldly bunch. Most of us dressed more modern. And the girls I was bringing were young and attractive and un-churchy looking. As the 'Doctor' faced the front in his black teaching gown; standing on his huge and high rostrum, our group of about 30 or 40 sat at his left side. Whenever he preached, he would express himself by using his hands. When he preached about heaven his right hand would go up and he would point heavenward or toward the ceiling with his fingers. When he preached about hell he would use his left hand and point downwards towards the floor where we sat. So although he preached assurance of salvation we would often feel like we were on a roller coaster of wondering whether we were really saved, especially during that time when he used his hand to express hell. When his right hand went up we felt good; when his left hand went down; we felt bad.

Even though I was committed to the work of the Lord I was still enjoying my social life to some extent. I found that most of the women at Westminster Chapel were very plain and dowdy looking. Also the place where I was trained, most of the girls there were older missionary types. It was called the Antioch and though we all attended the Chapel we were not officially connected or members. Every year we would invite the *'Doctor'* to come and speak to us. We didn't call him the *'doctor'* we were a little irreverent and called him *'Jonesy'* but not to his face. Although he didn't understand our methods as they and we were somewhat worldly, he was pleased to see us bringing more people to chapel each week. When I asked him about going dancing and meeting people he replied, "Make sure you are going for the right reasons. If it is to meet people to present the gospel that's fine, for you can touch members of society which I am never able to meet, but be cautious."

So during the week I would go out to dance, socialize and

witness; mainly to girls, but I also witnessed to some boys as well. It was funny to see the house in Kensington being decorated with pretty looking girls. Before I was converted I met Angela at a dance. We dated a couple of times. Sometime later I renewed our relationship and we dated regularly for quite a long time. When I became a Christian I told her what happened and she said she was thinking of becoming a Catholic.

At that time our relationship was not doing well and I was hoping that if she became a Christian then it would improve. Angela was a dancer and often played bit parts in movies. With the help of Derek we led her to the Lord. Soon she was bringing her friends from show business. To see them come down the aisle on Sunday morning at the chapel and observe some of the men on the top balcony leaning over and almost falling off watching the pretty girls especially when a number of them were models, dancers and starlets was quite amusing. At least it brought a bit of color to the drab surroundings. After several more months my relationship with Angela had become platonic and was going nowhere, so Derek advised me to break off the relationship which reluctantly I did. Within a few weeks she met a boy who owned a butcher's shop called John, led him to the Lord and within a few months they were married.

I met Kathie at a Saturday evening dance and gave her a ride home and made a date to take her for an afternoon drive the next day. We talked about all kinds of things and then she said she met this stupid guy that believed in Adam and Eve. When I said, I believed that as well, she was astounded. Around 5:30 pm I told her that I needed to drop her off home, as I was going to church and she wouldn't like it. She then asked why I thought she wouldn't like it? I replied that she wouldn't understand it. I had now insulted her intelligence so she was determined to prove me wrong by coming to church with me.

After the service which she didn't really understand, I took her back to the Antioch house to be fished. Timmy the actor witnessed to her and she finally said she would receive Christ and he gave her the booklet *'Beginning with Christ'* and told her learn the four verses and come to the baby basket. She had no intention of coming, but just said she would to get him off her back. When the actor got up, she heard him say to the director that she had made a commitment, but he didn't believe her and we probably wouldn't see her again. This made her angry so she decided to read the booklet, learn the verses and come to the baby basket to prove them wrong. I was due to go on holiday the next day so that meant she would have to make her own way to the Thursday evening beginner's class, which amazingly she did.

When I returned from my vacation, I found that Kathie had now become a Christian. During her reading of the booklet and attending the beginner's class she had come to believe it. I was very pleased, but I was now ready to pass Kathie onto the teachers and meet more girls to witness to, but that was not her idea. Kathie decided that she liked me and I had a responsibility to her. So we continued to date for quite a while. Eventually like most girls she wanted to know what my intentions were. I wasn't ready for a commitment; I just didn't know what I wanted at that time. Then she suggested that perhaps we should go to Australia for a couple of years because there was a program that one could sail there on a cruise ship for about $25.00. It was tempting, but you had to stay for two years otherwise you had to pay a full fare to return. I still wasn't sure, so Kathie finally went with a couple of girl friends instead.

Chapter Two
A Desire for Revival

During the time we attended Westminster Chapel we heard a lot of preaching on revival. Many of the visiting preachers gave us wonderful historic accounts of great revivals. Then they would say that's what we need and tell us what to do. We realized later that the problem was that none of them had personally experienced revival, it was all academic. No one can really preach about revival and shouldn't try unless they had been in a revival and had first hand experience.

When the Charismatic movement started around 1967 the curate (associate pastor) of All Souls Church, received the baptism of the spirit. All Souls at Langham Place, London was an Evangelical Anglican church; the popular senior pastor was John Stott. To complicate matters John Stott was adamantly against the movement, so it caused some waves amongst the evangelical community. Large crowds would go to All Souls on Sunday morning to hear John Stott preach and then go to Westminster Chapel on Sunday evening to listen to the *'Doctor.'* There was so much controversy that people were waiting to hear what the *'Doctor'* was going to say. Many people wanted him to condemn it, but he was very cautious. He wasn't opposed to the Charismatic movement, but he had some reservations. He believed in the spiritual gifts, including speaking in tongues. He argued that no movement is perfect and has problems, which is not a reason to dismiss the whole thing. He also said to those who say, "You were baptized in the spirit at salvation." "If that's true, then where is it?" He also complained that many reformed churches were so taken up with purity of doctrine, that they were spiritually dead. After I was filled with the spirit I realized that purity of heart was more important to God than purity of doctrine.

I had now bought a small pretty Georgian town house and I was gradually furnishing it as I had the money available. I was also missing Kathie and just at that time she contacted me either by phone or letter, saying she wanted to come home and could I send her some fare money, which I did. I met her at the docks with friends from the Antioch club and we were married six weeks later in November at Westminster Chapel with the Doctor performing the marriage service. It was not long after that time that Dr. Martyn Lloyd-Jones starting preaching on the baptism of the spirit for six months which was eventually put into a booklet called, *Joy Unspeakable.*

We all listened intently to his preaching; enjoying what he had to say, but in the end his Calvinism came out in such a way that it destroyed our faith, although we didn't realize it at the time. He finished the series of sermons by sighting many great Christian saints and reformers that had sought this wonderful experience. He said they were taken to a higher level and had such great joy and boldness that they hadn't experienced before. Many others sought diligently for years, but didn't find it. Then he said, "Seek the baptism with all your heart, but you may or may not receive it, because God is sovereign." So who were we to seek after this wonderful encounter? If the greats had sought so diligently and some of them hadn't received, how could we lesser mortals hope to qualify for this blessing?

We couldn't pray in faith, only in a vague hope. We were blinded to what Jesus had said, *"Ask and it will given to you; seek and you shall find; knock, and it will be opened to you."* (Mat.7:7) Jesus didn't say, *"Ask and it may be given, or it may not be given. Seek and you may or may not find. Knock and it may open, or it may stay closed."* That's what religious man says. We didn't know it at the time, but we were blinded by religious Calvinistic doctrines which closed our minds to the revelation of God's truth. They say they believe in prayer, but don't believe prayer changes things. They say you can only pray according to God's will and you can't make God change His mind as it's already set. As most of us never knew what God's perfect will was we would always end our prayers by saying, "If it be Thy will O Lord."

It seems to me that Calvinist preachers or teachers often emphasize the sovereignty of God in such a way as to fit in with their limited experience. They deduce things that bring certain conclusions, which put them in danger of going beyond where they should. For example they interpret that the scriptures reveal that it's all of God and none of man. Not all of man, or not part man and part God. Everything that happens to us is God's divine will and we cannot do anything to change it. It's a kind of fatalism which they just accept. God saves the elect and those that say, "We have the burden and responsibility to get people saved," are wrong, because we can't save anybody. The problem is that it's true, but it's not the truth. What most Calvinist do not understand, is that God primarily works through His church, (not like the old Roman Catholic teaching that salvation could only be found in the Catholic church) but God works through His people.

Jesus is the savior not me or you, but the '*Christ in us'* has the power to bring people into salvation. When Jesus was on earth God worked through a single man, (the Christ man) but even Jesus was limited, because He only had one tongue, one pair of hands and one pair of feet. But when He rose from the dead, the only begotten Son of God became the first born among many sons of God. Now the works of God could increase dramatically, because the true church had now become a body with many members. More anointed hands, feet and mouths to preach and perform the works of God. *"Go into all the world and preach the gospel to every creature. He who believes and is baptized will be saved; but he who does not believe will be condemned. And these signs will follow those that believe; "In my name" shall they cast out demons; they shall speak with new tongues; they shall cast away serpents; and if they drink any deadly thing, it shall not hurt them; they shall lay hands on the sick and they shall recover."* (Mk 16:15-17) Most religious churches can't handle those verses and conveniently delegated them to the original Apostles only and say only *'snake handling cults'* believe and practice those verses today.

No one knows everything about God and we shouldn't try to figure Him out with man-made doctrines. Making logical deductions and drawing conclusions which stretches scripture and goes beyond what God has revealed is dangerous. *"The secret things belong to the Lord our God, but those things which are revealed belong to us and our children forever, that we may do all the words of this law."* (Deut.29:29)

In other words, we don't reject truth, because if doesn't make sense to our religious intellect. We can only really know God through revelation and that's still limited, because He doesn't reveal everything to us, or to one specific group.

We often put ourselves in religious boxes; whether it's a big box, (part of a big denomination) or a small box, (a little church with a few that have the same beliefs) but it's still a box; then we're not open to others that aren't part of our box. In fact, we were so confident in our Calvinistic box that we were not interested in what others had to say. We had our interpretations, our spiritual books, and our reformed spiritual heroes. God was about to break our box, we just didn't realize it yet.

If you are a *'Johnny one note',* preacher, whether it's the *'Grace'* message the *'Salvation'* message the *'Messianic'* message, the *'Faith'* message the *'Prosperity'* message or any other aspect of God's truth, don't rob people from hearing the other aspects otherwise you and your hearers end up in '*error by emphasis.'* You are **not** their exclusive Shepherd. You are only an under-shepherd with lots of limitations. So to sum up God doesn't do it all, we cannot do it all, but God does it through His people. The Head needs a body as much as a body needs a head. A head is incomplete without a body as much as a body is incomplete without a head *"And He put all things under His feet, and gave Him to be Head over all things to the church which is His body the fullness of Him who fills all in all."* (Eph.1:22-23) A bridegroom needs a bride as much as a bride needs a bridegroom. Religious man is incomplete and will always be incomplete until his eyes are opened to the revelation of the purposes of God. He lives in measure until his eyes are open to see that he is called to fullness. *"For in Him dwells all the fullness of the Godhead bodily. And we are complete in Him."* (Col.2:9-10) God is into fullness. God is into completeness, isn't it amazing that God needs us as much as we need Him! You and I are very special, I know in the natural we are nothing, spiritually we are just a nobody, but when we are planted into His body then we become somebody; for we come into fullness, we become complete, not because of us, but because of Him. The gospel (good news) is greater and more magnificent than most believers comprehend. Not old sinners saved by grace, but saints; sons and daughters of the living God.

"Now to Him who is able to keep you from falling and to present you faultless before the presence of His glory with exceeding Joy. (Jude.24)

"Blessed be the God and Father of our Lord Jesus Christ who according to abundant mercy has begotten as again unto a living hope through the resurrection from Jesus Christ from the dead to an inheritance incorruptible and undefiled that fades not away reserved in heaven for you who are kept by the power of God through faith for salvation ready to be revealed in the last time." (1.Peter.1:3-5)

Another scripture we were blinded to was, *"For the Son of God, Jesus Christ, who was preached among you by us — by me, Silvanus, and Timothy — was not Yes and No, but in Him was Yes. For all the promises of God in Him are Yes, and in Him Amen, to the glory of God through us."* (2.Cor.2:19-20)

As previously mentioned, whenever we prayed, we always started or ended with saying, "If it be thy will O Lord," so mostly we didn't receive. Instead of checking to see if we had prayed in faith, or our motives were right, we always copped out by saying, "Perhaps it wasn't God's will."

"Let us therefore come boldly to the throne of grace that we might obtain mercy and find grace to help in time of need." (Heb. 4:16), wasn't what we were accustomed to doing. Neither did we expect our heavenly Father to give to us the Holy Spirit if we asked Him. After all we were not spiritual or deserving enough, which was crazy as that's just what we needed to become spiritual and more powerful. *"But you shall receive power when the Holy Spirit has come upon you; and you shall be witnesses to Me. . ."* (Acts.1:8)

"If you being evil know how to give good gifts to your children, how much more will your heavenly Father give the Holy Spirit to those who ask Him!" (Luke.11:13)

Another thing about Dr. Martyn Lloyd Jones was that he was a great admirer of the Puritans. Because of this we assumed that all Puritans were wonderful, dedicated, loving, Christians. So it took us many years to realize that this was not altogether true.

For example: The New England Puritans were not evangelists, having little interest in the salvation of anyone beyond their own fold. And they expected everyone who lived in New England to conform to their rules. Those who broke the rules, called transgressors, had eggs thrown at them in the stocks, were made to stand in the market place with notices attached to their foreheads describing their offenses, and were publicly whipped. Almost no offense against the Puritans rigid code of belief and behavior was too trivial for punishment. Terror and shame were used to encourage conformity even in the youngest. Boston minister, Cotton Mather, wrote, "are the souls of your children of no value... they are not too little to die, they are not too little to go to hell. In the preface of a children's book he thundered "Do you dare to run up and down upon the Lord's Day? Or do you keep in to read your book?" One of the few books found in ordinary households, besides the Bible and a catechism, was a long poem called *'The Day of Doom'* written by a minister called Michael Wigglesworth. One of its verses makes clear that unbaptized infants were dammed. However, God would allow them a measure of mercy.

> *A crime it is; therefore in bliss,*
> *You may not hope to dwell,*
> *But unto you I shall allow*
> *The easiest room in hell.*
>> Excerpts from "A Delusion of Satan." Frances Hill. Pages 10-11

Chapter Three
Revival Beginnings

Early one Saturday morning the door bell rang at our house. We had a late night before so we were still in bed. I went downstairs to see who it was. I opened the door and my old friend Ralph, who I had known for years and had led me to the Lord, was standing there. After he'd married he moved away and was no longer part of the Antioch crowd, also he no longer attended Westminster Chapel. We had been told by our leaders that he had gone off or had become strange.

"Ralph! What are you doing here?" I cried.

"The Lord sent me," he replied.

Kathie called down from upstairs, *"Who is at the door?"*

"It's Ralph! He said the Lord sent Him!" I replied.

"How did you find us?" I asked.

"I was visiting my mother and the Lord told me to come to see you. I didn't know where you lived and I didn't know that you were married or even lived in the area. I looked in a phone book and found you were close enough for me to walk to you."

I knew his mother lived less than a mile away, as I used to spend a lot of time at the house when Ralph lived there. "How did you find the way?" I asked. Our housing development was new and the address would be very hard to find.

"The Lord led me," he replied.

I knew immediately that he was on a much higher and different level that we were. By this time Kathie had come down and I was anxious to show Ralph our new pretty Georgian house and our Regency furniture, but he wasn't interested. He didn't beat about the bush.

"Have you received the Holy Spirit since you believed," he asked.

"No I haven't," I replied.

"Do you believe that God can fill you with the Holy Spirit?" he asked.

"Yes" I replied.

"Do you believe He will?"

"That's what I'm not sure about, I don't know if He will," I replied.

"You must believe He will," he stated.

"How will I know?" I asked.

He answered, *"When you believe, you will know,"*

Then he left. He didn't stay for a chit chat, a cup of tea, or anything. It was the strangest spiritual experience that I had ever had. Kathie thought he was really weird, but I had known Ralph a lot longer than Kathie and I knew he was genuine and sold out because that was the kind of person he was. Whenever he became really interested in something he would put his whole heart into it and so much the more, when it came to being a Christian.

After he was gone I decided to go up into my bedroom and give God a try. So as Kathie was busy in the kitchen, I went up and fell on my knees and asked God to fill me with the Holy Spirit. I told God that I believed, but help my unbelief. Suddenly I felt this hand gently pushing my head down towards the floor. Further and further it went almost touching the floor and that's when I became scared and stopped praying. But when I came down from the bedroom I was totally changed, and that's when my problems started.

I scared Kathie as I was so different and out of character. She grabbed her coat and was going to leave and go to her mom, but instead she began to call some of our Antioch friends and have some of them come to talk to me to sort me out. What happened then was that numbers of them began to be affected by what I was saying, so instead of them sorting me out, God was sorting them out. Even Derek was pleased, but said, *"Keep the blessing to yourself; don't rock the boat."*

Eventually we sold our house and bought a larger one. During that time we had nowhere to live as the second house was not ready for us to move into, so we stayed with Timmy the actor and his family for a few weeks. We began to pray for revival, also our hunger increased and we started to read other Christian books rather than the reformed ones which we were familiar with. During that time Timmy was often out of town working on a film or in a play, so he didn't participate in many of our prayer meetings. We began to break out of the Calvinistic mold. We began to read books by Watchman Nee, Andrew Murray, and Hannah Whitehall Smith. These were still old classics, but they seemed to have a lot more life and revelation in them than those old reformed theological teaching books.

Before, we would go to listen and critique the sermons. Visiting preachers would come when the Doctor was on vacation so we would compare each visiting preacher's sermons with the others and with the doctor's preaching. We were more interested on how good we thought the sermons were, rather than how much of the glory of God was upon the preachers. That isn't to say that most of them were not sincere, but some were certainly very religious. One man who came and preached at the chapel every summer was Leith Samuel from Southampton. He was lovely, spiritual, humble, gentleman. Unfortunately when revival eventually broke out in his church he vehemently opposed it.

After praying together for revival we seem to be stuck. We still were in a mixture of worldliness and spirituality. After we had prayed, Kathie and Timmy's wife Sheila would smoke a cigarette, have glass of whiskey or wine and then we would all watch the weekly horror movie on the TV. Finally I suggested that we should contact Ralph and purchase a train ticket for him to come and spend a few days with us. He lived in the west of England about a hundred and fifty miles away, he didn't have a car at the time, but he said he would come. He refused the offer of us buying him a train ticket, so he hitchhiked from the West Country to come and be with us which was in Barnes, a suburb of London.

A few days later Ralph arrived and we decided that he should stay for as long as was necessary. Timmy was away on a film job so Ralph, the three us, plus the kids were around. After the children were put to bed, we gathered for a prayer meeting. We sat down with our heads bowed in good evangelical tradition. Ralph was walking around the room with his hands in the air and his face lifted up. We didn't know what he was doing at first, but after about ten minutes we started to peep. We thought it was weird as this was outside our box; for most of the time he was behind us occasionally asking if we were getting anything. We hadn't a clue what he meant, as far as we were concerned we were praying; we were not expecting to get anything. We became very emotional which made us uncomfortable, as we were not Pentecostal, we didn't believe in yelling, crying, screaming, shaking, or swinging from the chandeliers.

After a while Shelia started to sob, a little while later, I began to tremble and also began to sob. Obviously something was happening, but we weren't sure what! It was a completely new experience. After that first meeting with Ralph things began to change. During his stay Ralph would often burst into song and start praising God. He mainly sang choruses and scriptures, which the children loved and we began to see how refreshing and different it was from the old-fashioned hymns we sang at the chapel.

A day or so later, Timmy came home. Because Ralph was staying, it was interfering with his routine. He had been away and he was now home for the weekend. Habitually, he would rise up early in the morning, go to the kitchen and make himself a cup of coffee; then take it into his front living room, put on his stereo and listen to his classical music records. But this Saturday morning Ralph was in the kitchen with the three kids making pancakes and marching around the kitchen all singing choruses. Timmy was so upset he decided to go out for breakfast. He returned an hour later complaining that he had suffered cold, greasy, eggs and had the worst breakfast in his life. God was obviously dealing with him.

Sunday morning he was still very grumpy. He asked if we were going to chapel that morning, but we decided we wanted to stay with Ralph and the kids and praise God in the house. He asked Ralph, why he didn't want to go to Westminster Chapel? Ralph answered, he'd had plenty of religion and now he was enjoying the life and he didn't want to return to the old realm. Timmy went off in a huff to Westminster Chapel for Sunday morning service. When he returned he was still upset. We had a glorious time with Ralph and we asked Timmy if he had enjoyed the service at the chapel. "Good teaching!" he said and changed the subject. Dr. Martyn Lloyd Jones had now retired as the pastor and different speakers were invited to come each Sunday and take the service, until the deacons could agree on which one of the speakers they should offer to become their new pastor.

After we had lunch, Ralph asked if he could talk to Timmy, so into the living room they went and locked the door. A couple of hours later they came out. Ralph had taken Timmy apart and he was a mess. Then he put him together again and there was now a change in him which gave him a hunger for more than religion. Like the rest of us, he was now hungry for new life and thirsty for new wine.

Now things were beginning to heat up, bearing in mind that Timmy was second in command at the Antioch place under Derek the director. People were hungry and we were excited. Ralph couldn't stay forever and went back home, but arranged for Ian to come from his church and stay with us at Timmy's house for a few days. Ian and his wife, Rosemary, also used to belong to the Antioch and went to the chapel. At that time we considered them to be very immature Christians; junior to us. Often they had marriage problems and wouldn't speak to each other. During those times they would often travel to the Sunday morning chapel service separately. Now we found out they had been totally transformed and were part of the church at Chard where Ralph was from. Ian now had a healing ministry and had great revelation.

We took great advantage of the situation when Ian and Rosemary came to stay and invited all our friends to come to the house meetings. Everyone was being delivered and filled with the Spirit. It was amazing to see how a person depressed and forlorn would enter the room where Ian was ministering and ten minutes later they would appear radiant and joyful.

Frank's wife Anita went in and came out so changed that Frank was very upset. He said, "That's not my wife, what have they done to her?" He walked the streets for two hours with another brother Mike who was so flabbergasted he didn't know what to say or how to respond. He ended up saying to Frank in their walk, *"Have you read any good books lately?"* Later Mike said that he couldn't handle what was happening, because it was so out of his experience, so he got relief by changing the subject.

Chapter Four

Encountering Opposition & Coming into Freedom

Over the next few weeks about one third of the Antioch members came into an amazing experience with the Lord. We all still were officially members of the Antioch and Derek and his wife were concerned with what was happening. Timmy was now out of town filming a movie so he wasn't available. Derek called a meeting asking me to come and give an account of myself. So I went with the others and testified. I didn't say I had been filled with the spirit. I knew nothing about speaking in tongues; they weren't the issues.

What I was saying is that you could live a victorious life and didn't have to keep sinning and struggling every day. That Jesus not only came to save us and deliver us from the penalty of sin, but also from the power of sin. When I quoted the scriptures, *"Sin shall not have dominion over you. If you walk in the spirit you shall not fulfill the lusts of the flesh,"* it was like a red rag to a bull. They were protesting and saying we sin and continue to sin all the time. Even when we pray we sin. "*We were born in sin and shaped in iniquity."* We were all miserable sinners saved by grace. They couldn't see that we were saved from being miserable sinners to become saints. They only believed that happened when we got to heaven, but meanwhile we live in constant defeat. One person said it sounded too good to be true that you could live in victory. Derek couldn't really give me any New Testament scriptures to back up his position. It was the first time he didn't know what to say. It seemed at the time that he was somewhat open to what I was saying and even thanked me for sharing and said they had a lot to think about. But his wife Marion was very adamant that I was wrong and was totally opposed. Soon after I left the meeting he officially closed the Antioch and then re-opened it again, barring all of us who had been blessed from coming.

After forbidding anyone to have anything do to with us (including Kathie's brother) we decided that it wouldn't be appropriate for us to return to Westminster Chapel even though Martyn Lloyd-Jones had retired as pastor after 35 years and was now writing and doing some itinerant preaching. Later I did contact the current pastor, Glen Owen, a Welsh preacher who took over from the Doctor and gave him my testimony. He didn't know what to say and couldn't refute what I said, even though he didn't like my testimony or anything to do with spiritual gifts.

Sometime later Ralph invited Kathie and me to come down to his church for a weekend. It was in a little village called South Chard in the county of Somerset in the West of England. Dick and Carol a young married Baptist couple had received this blessing and came with us on the 150 mile trip from the London area.

Angela the ex-girlfriend of mine who I had led to the Lord called and warned me about going to that church. She said, *"I know someone who knows of someone, who visited that church. The people there have thrown their Bibles out of the window, the children are crawling under the pews looking for Jesus; blind people keep bumping into each other saying, 'I can see! I can see!' Strange music comes out of the walls and they have colored flashing lights during the service."*

As we were driving down I remember saying to Dick and Carol, *"I might be able to handle most things, but I'm not sure about the colored flashing lights."*

Angela did eventually visit South Chard.

We arrived a few hours later at Ralph and Michelle's house. They were both so pleased to see us. The first thing that Kathie noticed was a tambourine hanging on a hook which freaked her out. She was thinking, after Westminster Chapel, a church with tambourines was too much. After all this was not the Salvation Army. We had just arrived in time for dinner. Ralph led the blessing for the meal and the anointing fell on him and he started praising and worshiping God. Then Michelle fell under the anointing also and after about forty minutes we were ready to eat; which was much to my disappointment as the food was now cold. During the meal several friends from the church popped in to say hello. On elderly titled lady that lived in a manor house, came in literally skipping and shouting *"Hallelujah! Hallelujah!"* and testifying of the miracles that had happened to her that day.

After the meal, Ralph took us into the little front room so he could pray and minister to us before the Saturday night meeting at the church. He was going around asking each of us, if we had been filled with the Spirit? Then he would ask if we could speak in tongues? Most of us hadn't, but he hadn't reached me yet. I left the room and found a little empty room and thought if I have been filled with the Spirit I should be able to speak in tongues, so I opened my mouth and began to speak out a heavenly language.

I then went back into the room where Ralph was still ministering and sat down. He eventually came up to me and asked me if I was filled with the Spirit? To which I replied, *"Yes."*

He then asked if I spoke with tongues and I answered, *"Yes!"*

Then he asked me, *"When?".*

I replied, *"A few minutes ago."* .

He shouted, *"Praise the Lord!"*

Later that evening we all went to the evening meeting. First of all, there were no colored flashing lights, no music coming out of the walls, Bibles were not being thrown out of the windows, children were not crawling under the seats looking for Jesus and blind people were not bumping into each other claiming that they could see.

What was different was there wasn't a pulpit. There was a platform, but the children were sitting on it. Apparently the Lord had told the pastor to get rid of the pulpit and have open body ministry. There was a modern organ in one corner and the seating was arranged in a large square. There was a lot of praise and worship with the children singing and playing tambourines. They sang mainly scriptures and choruses and many people were dancing some with their eyes closed. The praise was intermingled with visions, prophesies, words of knowledge, and testimonies. Even some of the children gave out words, prophesies, and visions. Several messages were preached as different preachers stood up in the middle and many people's needs were met.

Sunday morning we were back again for the next meeting. I remember one preacher got up and as he preached his face shone like gold with the glory of the Lord. The message was life giving. Having attended Westminster Chapel for ten years, I had sat under some of the greatest reformed preachers in the world, but nothing like this; there was no comparison; it was like being in heaven. Most of the time you couldn't see the pastor, no one had prominence it was only Jesus. When the pastor did speak he stood on a chair in a corner (he was a little man) and talk about how lovely and wonderful Jesus was and tears would flow down his face. Many people would get delivered as he spoke. His was affectionately known as Uncle Sid and his short rosy cheeks wife, known as Auntie Mill.

There was this small church out in the middle of South Chard, a little village and people were coming from everywhere, even from overseas. People wanted to move there just to be in the flow of what God was doing. They had seven full time ministers that traveled up and down the country and abroad. None of them were paid a salary, but they all lived by faith. The people there also met from house to house. Everyone greeted each other with a 'Holy Kiss,' which was very strange to us at first. Spontaneous house meetings were happening all the time, as well as the Saturday night and Sunday morning and evening meetings in the church building.

Almost everyone would eat Sunday lunch in the dining hall after the Sunday morning meeting. Auntie Mill and some of the sisters prepared the food. She never knew how many would be staying for lunch. Most of the time there were more people arriving than she had food prepared for. Yet miraculously she was always able to feed everyone with plenty. It was like a re-enactment of the loves and fishes. After the lunch was over many would worship the Lord around the kitchen sink as they were washing the dishes by hand.

Because many people could not travel there on a regular basis it spawned the house church movement. From time to time their ministers came and ministered to different groups of Christians that began to meet in houses. It began to network all over England. Songs from the Lord would be shared. Revelation and ministry were imparted. The ministry was supported and blessed and people gave as the Lord prompted. Other streams also were opening up, commonly known as the House Church movement.

Chapter Five
Moving Into Our New House & Area

By this time Kathie and I had moved into our new house we began to have meetings. We met on a Tuesday night and people began to come, retired missionaries, students, families with kids. We would visit different local churches on Sunday and meet people who were hungry. They would come or were brought to one of our meetings and this became their lifeline. Their churches for the most part were very small and dead.

Our duplex house was packed with as many as 70 people and we were not quiet and the meetings were long and people were getting baptized in the bath and getting delivered in the woodshed. Our next door neighbors were Baptist and were having a hard time with the noise and all the people coming. Also the church in Chard was sending people to us that lived in the London area. They had accommodation in their church for people to stay and some arrived saying that the leaders at Chard had told them we would put them up. We had to let them know we were limited with the room we had available.

Our neighbors complained and the local zoning official knocked on our door saying it was reported that our house was being used as a hostel, when he ask, "If this was true?" Kathie replied, "No! It's just my brothers and sisters visiting." So he apologized and left. Of course they were our spiritual brothers and sisters. There were so many hungry people we began to meet on Thursday evenings as well which became a further problem to our Baptist neighbors. We knew we would soon have to find a larger place to meet.

In England most people never attended church. Many of the church buildings had closed and been sold and were now Mosques. We were not interested in building mega-churches as they do in the US, as we wanted the fellowships to stay reasonable small, so relationships could grow and body ministry could flourish. We didn't want people to be lost or just hide in a crowd. We wanted to have plenty of them, not just in our town, but in many towns all over the British Isles.

We had the New Testament vision of the early church. We believed in community, but not communes. There were some groups, usually young people that gathered in communes and shared their children and their clothes and lived in camps. We felt that was dangerous and it proved to be true. Most of them ended up as dangerous cults like the *"Children of God."* In fact, the leader of that movement's daughter whose name was Faith came to our house with a few of her disciples and ministered. She was very impressive and radical and preached with tears running down her face as she seemed so sold out.

Fortunately, Ralph was visiting us at that time and he

discerned a pride and exclusive spirit on them and warned us to be careful. One of our young men Stuart who was an art student, went off with them and they re-named him Gabriel and he was living in a commune and ministered on the streets in Amsterdam, until he came to his senses and managed to leave and return to us after about a year.

During that time when Ralph was with us a young intellectual, female, student, who was a Jewish Atheist was brought to him and was ready to debate as she was very hostile to Christians. Ralph just exposed her whole life to her including her hatred of her father, by operating in the *'Word of Knowledge'* and she fell apart and became a believer.

Kathie's Office Testimony

I had worked for Jewish companies most of my life. David's family is part Jewish (his Jewish dad grew to love Jesus and was saved in his sleep). At this point I had returned from Australia and had married David and I was working for a Jewish Fashion House in London. I was the national cash register supervisor in the accounts department. The company was very worldly but strongly Jewish. I had been somewhat worldly until I was filled with the Holy Spirit and that had been recently.

I never had a testimony where I worked, because I was about as worldly as the rest of them. I knew that soon I would be leaving. There was so much going on with the revival that we literally did not have time to go to work. There were so many people coming from everywhere. David had now left his job and was living by faith.

So I said to the Lord, "You know God when I leave here I want to leave with a testimony so that these people know you are alive."

"You will!" He said, "Just do what I tell you and I will give you a testimony."

"Yes Lord that sounds good."

To be honest I thought God might give a few little prophecies like, "God really loves you." Or "God wants you to know He will take care of you." Well I was in for a shock, because that's not what I got. In UK people are usually much more timid and aren't very loud about sharing their faith. It's not "accepted" as in America. A lot of Christians don't pray publicly in the restaurants as it's kind of weird to other people. I remember a friend of mine trying to be brave and making a stand, bowing his head and praying over his food at the lunch table at work. After a while one of his co-workers said to him, "Richard, why do you sniff your food like that before you eat it?"

So I started talking about the Lord and started humming a chorus and they would hum the same chorus. Then I would start to sing the words to the chorus, "Jesus taste like honey in the rock," and they would sing the words and then get mad when they realized what they were doing. The next thing that happened was that there was a flu epidemic and everyone in our office was planning to get shots.

Mr. Joseph, the chief accountant, said to me, "We are all going to get our shots now."

"No thanks" I'm not going," I replied.

"You don't understand these shots are 90% proof." He stated.

"Well mine is a 100% proof."

They all went off to get their shots and when they returned my eyes started to water and I began to sniff with cold symptoms. At 5:00 pm as we were leaving for the day they all laughed and said, "Well we will see you in two weeks."

When I arrived home I was feeling really bad so I asked David to pray for me and he laid his hands on me and prayed and I was instantly healed. When I arrived back at work the next morning in perfect health they ignored me as though I wasn't there.

The next thing that happened after I said I would do what God said was this: The head salesman came into my office looking for the Chief Accountant.

As he came in the Lord began to tell me something, "Tell him that He is stealing the company accounts (customers) and selling them to another company and then he's fixing to follow them."

"Oh wow I will pray for him" I thought.

"Tell him" said God."Perhaps you could tell him Lord. After all he is one of Yours," meaning that he was Jewish. God was silent so I knew I had to make a decision.

"Oh, excuse me" I said. He came to my desk and I told him what God had showed me. He looked like cat with its tail in the electric socket. "How do you know this?" he said staring at me.

"God told me" I replied.

"What are you going to do?" he asked.

"I won't do anything if you bring all the customers back" I replied.

Needless to say, he did just that.

Next one was the Chief Accountant himself. The Holy Spirit said to me one day "He is stealing large amounts of money from the petty cash and "expense accounts."

"Oh well what can you do?" I thought. "He can only get mad and fire me." I went into his office. He looked at me. I told him what God told me with a few more details. He also went white he was very white already with red hair which he was now pulling. "What are you going to do?" he asked me, thinking his goose was cooked.

"I won't do anything if you bring back as much money as you can and promise never to ever to do that again because God knows everything." He didn't need reminding.

It went on like this for a while and people were scared to come into my office. They walked way around me. God said He would show me where the balances were out if I believed. Everyone at the end of the month would be spending hours trying to find balances that were out and didn't reconcile. I made a statement. "I will not have to spend time looking for balances that are out at the end of the month because God is going to show me where it's out." People looked at me, but didn't say anything.

At the end of the month, I could see they were waiting to see what was going to happen. As usual all our balances were out. I know that in the natural there was no quick way to do this, so I didn't even begin to look. The other people in the office were looking at me out of the corner of their eye. I just sat and waited a couple of minutes.

"Look in the "H" section at the front" the Holy Spirit said.

So I did and there it was - my difference. I just corrected it and went on working. No one said anything!

The same kind of thing happened over and over. No one cussed or said bad things around me. Truly these people were scared of what God knew about them. It didn't make them become Christians at that point, but they sure knew He was REAL.

After several months I left because there was just too much happening in the revival to have time to go to work. The revival was bringing people from everywhere.

But the icing on the cake for me was an incident that happened about three months after I had left. I was at home when the telephone rang. It was the Chief Accountant, Mr. Joseph.

"Hello", he said, "we have a problem that you may be able to help us with; could you come back to the office? We will pay you whatever you like."

I finally agreed and negotiated a good amount as I am not a dummy.

"What is it?" I asked.

"We have had this balance out for 2 months and we can't find it and even the auditor can't find it. So we thought maybe you could ask, 'Him up there?'"

Well you could have knocked me down with a feather. That was a major miracle for him to acknowledge God. I didn't want to pass up an opportunity for God to show off His great abilities. And I made a date to go the following week.

The next week when I got the train to London I was asking the Lord to show me right away where the balance was. I got to the office and they had a desk all set up. It was piled high with large posting sheets which were all covered in hundreds of small printed figures. In the natural there is no way anyone can find that mistake without pouring through everything and you are looking at a week's worth of work. Everyone in the office tip-toed around as though they didn't want to disturb God; they also spoke very quietly. They were watching me out of the corner of their eye. I sat down and took a deep breath. I knew they were waiting me for to pray. Well I didn't need to pray as I already prayed, but I obliged and bowed my head for a minute.

Under my breath I was saying. "Lord there's no way I can even look at this you will have to tell me." By faith I began to turn over the pages because it was almost impossible to search for it. I just tuned in to the Lord and turned the pages slowly. People could see that I wasn't even really looking. After I turned over the pages for about three minutes the Holy Spirit spoke to me, "Its right there" He said. I looked down and there it was, right in the middle of the page! "Here it is" I said. They looked at me and someone said, "We knew He could find it." As far as I know at that time none of those Jewish people were saved, but they sure did know that God was alive and well. He had their number! And I had a testimony.

Chapter Six
Our Faith Increases

As we started looking for a larger place to worship we heard of a local church which only had a congregation of about four people. Somehow we got to visit the pastor who said he was hungry for revival. He had heard about what was happening with us and said he wanted to see something similar. I explained to him that his church building could be filled within weeks as God was really moving to those who were open to His Spirit. Unfortunately, his hunger was for a revival of historic 'Calvinism'; but that was no longer an issue, it wasn't what the Holy Spirit was doing. We gave him an option, but after praying he declined and he lost his church and it eventually closed down.

We were now packed with people at our house and began to pray and ask others to pray to see if we could find a larger place to meet. Within two days one of the girls felt led to go to the center of our local town which was where the market was held and ask if they had a room in the building there. They did and it was available. We had found a hall right in the middle of the town surrounded by four churches. It was the Market hall right there in the center of Town that was known as the 'Apple Market.' The hall held a little over a hundred people so we changed our Thursday night home meeting to this hall. You must bear in mind back then most local churches never had more than 25-30 people on a Sunday. Later we outgrew that hall and eventually found another hall that could accommodate about 200 people, but I don't want to get ahead of the story.

We started out meeting on Thursday evenings and visited different churches on Sundays. Thursday evening meetings began to explode and people were coming and being changed and blessed, but then they were going back to their old dead churches for Sundays. Eventually we felt that the Lord wanted us to meet on Sunday morning at the Market hall as well. Fortunately it was available.

People then had to make a decision whether to continue to traditionally go their old church, or fellowship with us on Sunday mornings. The serious ones did and only a few couldn't break from the loyalty they had to their old dead churches. Sunday evenings we had four house meetings. Many visitors were flocking to the Sunday morning meetings and we would announce if they really wanted to know what we were about they were invited to our houses for Sunday lunch with an option of staying for the evening house meetings. We had to find lots of extra beef or chicken and vegetables to feed our visitors Sunday lunch and many became part of our fellowship.

In the Tuesday and Sunday evening house meetings we

were still learning to move in the spirit. When we see what goes on in many churches today, we remember how God set us free during that time from those religious mindsets and religious ways of doing things. We discovered a whole new concept of "church meetings" and worship and worship teams. What God did then He can still do today. On Sunday morning in the hall, when it was time for the offering, we didn't pass around a collection plate. We didn't leave a box by the exit. We didn't have someone get up and teach on tithing or giving.

As we started to praise and dance, someone would push a container on a table to the middle of the hall and people would walk or dance around it. As they were led, they would give; not just into the container, but also to each other. Money flowed freely and as people were led by the Holy Spirit every need was met. Often people would come with no money for the week's groceries or to pay their gas or electric bill, but during that time they would leave with enough. Nobody would share their needs, yet so many times the giving to a person in need was exactly the right amount.

One time during the offering the Lord told Kathie to put ten pounds in the offering container. She looked and found she didn't have her purse. Suddenly someone put two pounds in her hand she knew it was not enough to put in the offering. So she prayed and gave it to someone else, then someone put five pounds in her hand, she took it and as she was led she gave it to another. Just after that someone put ten pounds in her hand. She said, "thank you Jesus." And put it into the offering container. As the meeting came to an end and we were leaving someone put twenty pounds in her hand. One Sunday morning someone felt that the Lord wanted us to bless the children financially. We took an offering and shared out the money equally to the children much to their delight. The following Sunday morning it was standing room only, because loads of our kid's friends had arrived. On Monday our children told their friends at school what had happened in the Sunday morning meeting. Somehow a rumor went around that we gave away free money to kids every Sunday.

Another time we gave away ten pounds in the meeting, which was our weekly grocery money. There was a visitor on that Sunday morning who was a member of an Assembly of God Pentecostal Church. On the Monday he phoned and asked if he could come by to our house and talk to us. As we sat down and had tea (which is an English tradition) he told us how he was amazed and so impressed with the meeting. He said he had never seen anything like it. He was a little older than us and his name was Roy and he was an insurance salesman.

After we talked and shared for a while, he said he had to go and just as he was leaving he asked if 'ten' meant anything to us. We looked and said it could do. He opened his wallet and counted out ten one pounds notes and said the Lord directed him to give us this. When we shared how we have given away our grocery money on Sunday he was thrilled. Roy became part of the fellowship and was a close friend of ours.

A little later we gave our grocery money away which was ten

pounds. We had a couple who were members of the Salvation Army visiting us at our house. They were fascinated with the way we were living by faith. The postman had just come and Kathie went to open up a letter saying, "Thank you Lord for our grocery money." Inside the letter read "I felt the Lord told me to send you this." It was ten pounds; the Salvation Army couple was astounded.

At that time we had one well-off man that came to the meetings. He had his own business. One Sunday morning several people felt lead to give him money and they couldn't understand why. Everything in the natural didn't make sense. "He doesn't need money he is very prosperous." But people were learning to hear the Spirit of God and to obey. When he was given these monetary gifts he began to cry. The Lord had told to give all his income that his business had brought in that week to one of the saints that was in desperate need so he obeyed. His wife didn't even have cash for groceries, (this was before the credit card was invented) but he experienced, *"But my God shall supply all your needs according to His riches in Glory by Christ Jesus."* (Phil.4:19)

We were all learning that the greater included the lesser. *"He that spared not His own son but delivered Him up for us all, how shall He not with Him also give us freely all things?"* (Rom.8:32) We saw that if we could trust God with our eternal destiny through Jesus Christ, then we must also be able to trust God with our temporal needs. Bill the butcher was another brother that came regularly to the fellowship and often he would bring sausages for us. There was a real sense of community; it was the New Testament in action.

When Kathie went shopping in our main town of Kingston upon Thames she would look in the window of the gas showrooms. They had brand new sparkling cookers - gas cookers and ovens and stoves. She noticed one in particular that she just loved- it was blue and white and it had a DOUBLE OVEN side by side. She thought it was the neatest thing - but it was expensive and she felt she could live without it.   Although she still looked at it all the time.

Next Sunday she was sitting in the meeting and God was moving. A brother in the meeting, Barry, stood and gave out a word of knowledge. He said God wanted us to ask for something from Him that was in our heart. God loves to give gifts to children you know. He said when we knew what it was to stand to our feet.

Of course the first thing that came to Kathie's mind was that wonderful cooker with the double oven. She was about to stand up and as she did her eyes looked upon a friend across the room. Doreen had confided in her that week that more than anything else she wanted a visitation from God. So by the time Kathie was standing she had decided that for her "wish" she would ask for the blessing for Doreen and never mind about the oven.

When she stood and we prayed, that's what she asked for, "A visitation from Doreen and a blessing for her life."

She sat down and the man next to her leaned over and said,

"When you stood up I had a vision of your kitchen."

"Really" she said.

"Yes it was the strangest vision. I was in your kitchen and it had a big blue and white double oven gas cooker."

Of course she burst out laughing! Sometime later a person came to our house and asked if there was something that she really wanted. Kathie mentioned the oven. Needless to say it wasn't long before Kathie got her oven. God is generous, kind and wonderful.

Kathie was sitting at home with a friend and she made a list of groceries that she needed to buy as some people were coming to stay for the weekend. She looked in her purse but had no money. So she thought we will go anyway and they both started to walk towards the local supermarket at the end of the high street. They were holding the shopping bags and singing a chorus, suddenly they heard footsteps running from behind.

A woman from our fellowship grabbed her arm and said, "I was traveling on the bus and I looked out of the window and saw both of you walking towards the high street with your shopping bags. The Holy Spirit told me to get off the bus right away and give you some money for your shopping."

The money she gave us was enough to buy, not only the food, but extra for deserts for our guests.

We had a number of ex-missionary ladies that were committed to the fellowship and were a wonderful blessing. Doreen blessed us many times as she gave generously to us by the spirit which enabled us to pay our mortgage or go overseas on mission trips. When we left permanently for the US we were able to bless her by leaving her our car.

Chapter Seven
Ever Increasing Faith

Harry Greenwood was one of the ministers at Chard and had a wonderful faith ministry and had seen many miracles happening in healing and provision. He said when he first started praying for the sick the first three people he prayed for died and he wondered if he had a ministry of death. Then he said, "I'm not going to stop, even if everyone dies, because the Bible says they shall lay hands on the sick and they shall recover. And by His stripes we were healed." It wasn't long before he had an amazing miracle and healing ministry.

One Sunday morning at Chard, Harry stood up and began to minister. He preached a faith message on receiving answers to your prayers. He was explaining that it is not enough to pray in faith, but we must also receive the answers through faith. He was preaching from the passage in Mark where Jesus said, *"Therefore I say to you whatever things you ask when you pray, believe that you receive them. And you will have them."* (Mark.11:24) There was a woman in the meeting who went to the Chard fellowship regularly, but her husband had no interest. She was praying for his salvation, but somehow nothing was happening. The woman stood up for her unsaved husband and asked for prayer and agreement that he would receive salvation. Harry prayed then told her to go home and rejoice that her husband was now saved even though she could see no physical evidence. When she went to bed that night as her husband fell asleep she looked at him and said, "Little do you know that you are saved."

The following Sunday morning as she was getting ready for church, he suddenly said, "I'm coming with you." He said later that the reason he decided to come with her to church was because he didn't want to stay at home and cook the Sunday lunch.

He then went on to say that when he got to the church the people looked ordinary to him and nothing special about them. However, when the meeting started and the people and children began to worship, dance, and play tambourines he was taken aback. Especially by the joy on their faces.

After a while he suddenly began to see a bright light at the end of the church and a figure began to advance towards him. At the same time he was moving closer to the figure and he was looking down and saw these sandaled feet. He slowly raised his eyes and saw a shining white gown as he lifted his eyes further the light became brighter and brighter. He lifted his eyes up as far as the shoulders and beard of the person, but then it was so bright he couldn't look any higher because the light was blinding. So he never saw the face. He lowered his eyes, trembling and shaking and weeping and the vision slowly disappeared. This was all happening during the worship and he was gloriously saved. He began to cry out and speak in other tongues and worship and for several days he devoured the scriptures and his life was totally transformed. Some time later, he became a faithful deacon in the church and that's when we met him and his precious wife.

When we learned of this we decided to see if it would work for us. My dad was a nice Jewish man, but didn't practice his religion. I was concerned about his salvation and had witnessed to him several times even with tears. My mother was a little Catholic lady and thought that salvation was earned by living a good life and attending mass. Kathie's mother was a nice respectable lady, but felt religion or church going was for wicked or sinful people which she was not. So Kathie and I prayed together and agreed for their salvation according to what Jesus said in Mark 11. Then we kept thanking Him.

The first thing that happened was that my dad was saved in his sleep. According to my mom he woke her up in bed in the middle of the night. His eyes were closed his hands were raised in the air and he was crying out, "Jesus my Messiah." When he awoke in the morning he was saved. He bought a Bible and faithfully attended our meetings. I even had the privilege of baptizing him in our bath.

I had arranged for my Dad and Mom to come with us to Chard. It was the Saturday night meeting and my mother was apprehensive. There was a Roman Catholic Priest a German theologian; a professor of comparative religion at the meeting. He was in London and was hungry for a greater spiritual experience. Someone invited him to Chard and arranged for him to stay with Andrew Jordan a spirit filled Baptist preacher who lived at Chard and was part of the fellowship.

I said to my mother, "That man over there is a Catholic Priest; just keep your eyes on him. If he is happy with the meeting you know it will be fine." The meeting started with praise and dancing and tambourines. After about ten minutes the priest suddenly stood up gave out a blood curdling scream and ran down the isle falling on his back, knocking chairs all over the place. He had been involved in séances and hypnotism; and he was getting delivered.

My mother jumped up and cried, "They are killing the Priest," and run out of the building. I followed her down the road trying to catch her up and calm her down, but I couldn't get her back into the meeting for love or money. I eventually escorted her back to her room where she was staying and went back to the meeting to see the priest climbing out of the baptismal tank, prophesying, speaking in tongues, and laying hands on people and they were still worshiping. My Dad loved it and thought it was awesome.

My mother eventually came to an outreach healing and salvation meeting that we hosted in our home town for Harry Greenwood. She was prayed for and was healed and that got her attention. She then raised her hand for salvation as Harry preached the gospel. She loved to tell of her experience at Chard and would laugh at her reaction. Even though she stayed a Catholic and still attended mass she would come to all the Holy Ghost meetings she could and she loved them. Roy often took her to revival meetings when we weren't around. She often complained that her Sunday church mass were dead and dry or the priest was boring.

Kathie's mother was a little different. She was in her seventies and was a widow and she was behaving out of character, because normally she was always a fairly gentle lady. We had taken her to Chard to a meeting and it had freaked her out. She couldn't get the choruses that were sang out of her head and thought she was going mad. So now she was very hostile towards us, and said, "Don't expect me to visit you when you end up in a mental institution." Every time she called she exploded, but I encouraged Kathie to just kept thanking God for her salvation.

After a couple of months she phoned Kathie and said, "I don't know what to do tomorrow," which was a Sunday.

Kathie replied, "Why don't you visit your sister Grace."

"I don't want to do that. All she ever does is talk about people and criticize them."

"Why don't you watch television?" asked Kathie.

"All they have on is rubbish," she replied.

"Go and see a movie," suggested Kathie.

"You shouldn't go the movies on a Sunday," she replied indigently.

It was funny, she wasn't a churchgoer, but she had a religious hang-up about Sundays. Kathie then said, "I don't know what to tell you!'

She replied, "I thought I might come to one of your meetings."

"You wouldn't like it Mom."

"Don't tell me what I wouldn't like. How do you know what I like?" she replied.

"OK!" said Kathie, "I'll ask Roy to pick you up in the morning."

That was it, she came and eventually got baptized and faithfully came to the fellowship. Her life was changed. She came out of her shell and started going on trips and tours and seeing parts of the world that she had never dreamed existed.

We remember being in a meeting at South Chard and the glory of God was there. A visiting Pastor (Doug) was in the meeting. Funnily enough he had preached about "Body Ministry" for years, but when it was happening before his eyes he got upset. God was moving on the body and people were prophesying and singing songs from the Lord and all he could say was, "Where is the pastor? Who is in charge? Where is the leader? Why is there no 'front'?"

Well the pastor would sit in a corner and cry about how beautiful Jesus was. If God moved on him to speak or share he would have to climb onto a chair and stand so that people could see where the voice was coming from. He would talk about Jesus and everyone would cry (or laugh). This little man was less than five feet tall, but he would hug people and demons would fly out of them, for he was so full of the love of Jesus.

Doug was getting angry because it didn't seem that anyone was in control. Well of course the Holy Spirit was in control, but Pastor Doug didn't know the Holy Spirit well enough to know that. After the meeting was over Pastor Doug went searching for the pastor demanding to know why he wasn't at the front taking control of the meeting and preaching with a pulpit? The little pastor carried on eating his lunch and never responded. Pastor Doug ended up staying for the evening meeting that something was drawing him, of course, even though he was mad. In the evening one of the evangelists got up and said that there were ten people in the meeting who were supposed to be baptized in water. We had a tremendous revelation of water baptism and saw many people healed and delivered when they went into the water.

We saw how it's a burial service and the old man (nature) is buried with Him (Jesus) in Baptism. Rom. 6. Also the mode of baptism, unlike traditional churches that baptize in the name of the Father, in the name of the Son, and in the name of the Holy Spirit, they baptized in the name of the *Lord Jesus Christ*. The position was that the name of the Father is not a name, but a title. For example, if I baptized someone in my father's name, (which is Michael) then I would say I baptize you in the name of Michael. So to baptize in the name of the Father is to baptize in the name of Jehovah/Adonai which is translated 'Lord' in English. To baptize in the name of the son is 'Jesus' and to baptize in the name of the Holy Spirit can only be 'Christ' the Anointed one. There are no names given to the Holy Spirit. In the book of Acts every time they baptized it was either done in the name of the Lord, or in the name of Jesus, or in the name of Christ. They cast out demons and healed the sick and it was **not** done by saying, "in the name of the Father, Son, and Holy Ghost." *"Whatever you do in word or deed do all in the name of the Lord Jesus giving thanks to God the Father through Him."* (Col.3:17)

So what they believed and practiced was not about splitting hairs, but they believed that there was supernatural power in that name. And they proved it as many miracles happened when people were baptized. *"At the name of Jesus, every knee should bow of those in heaven and those on earth and those under the earth, and every tongue shall confess that Jesus Christ is Lord, to the glory of God the Father."* (Phil. 2:10-11) *"For in Him dwells all the fullness of the Godhead bodily."* (Col.2:9)

Because of this revelation we saw many miracles happen in water baptism. David Moxen a minister we knew said that if water baptism is a symbolic burial then it results in a symbolic victory. But we were witnessing real victories as the old man was buried. Alex was a lonely Scots lad that we led to the Lord at the Antioch. He had come from the world and had been a heavy smoker. Although he was now a Christian he was still addicted to three packs of cigarettes a day. When we baptized him he came out of the water saying, "I have a funny taste in my life." It was the taste of a non-smoker. He never had any desire to smoke again.

He soon met a sweet girl named Mary and eventually they got married. Both of them continued living as radiant Christians. Timmy's younger daughter who was about eight suffered with a kidney infection. They were visiting Chard and she wanted to be baptized. They were concerned about her getting into the cold water with her infection and also didn't know why she wanted to do it. They felt she just wanted to copy others, so when they asked her she said, "When I go into the water the old nature will be buried and I will come up in Christ and He doesn't have kidney problems so neither will I." As they helped her into the tank someone touched her side and she screamed out in pain, but when she came up out of the water she was totally healed.

So back to Pastor Doug, after a while there were nine people who had responded to this invitation. The evangelist said, "We will wait for God to speak to the last person." Pastor Doug's heart began to beat faster. "You can't mean me, surely Lord? I have been a pastor for 30 years I can't go and get baptized in this strange church." But there was silence and Doug was very uncomfortable.

At the front of the church, written on the wall was a painting of a cross and a banner wrapped around it which said, "The Truth will set you free." Doug prayed quietly to God, "Lord if you want me to be baptized you will need to write it on the wall like the sign. No one else needs to see it, just me." Just then an elderly lady across the other side of the church jumped up and began to prophesy, "Why are you asking God to write it on the wall when He has already written it on the tables of your heart?" Well Pastor Doug froze and beads of sweat run down his forehead. How did that lady know what he was saying in his heart? Of course she didn't know, but she could hear from God and the Holy Spirit dropped that into her spirit and she just prophesied what she heard God tell her. Doug finally realized that everything he had been preaching about, God using the Body of Christ and the Body edifying itself was happening right there and he was right in the middle of it. He jumped up and was baptized. His life and ministry were totally changed when he saw the Holy Spirit moving in and on every member. We don't think there is anything as exciting as when the church (living stones) are Spirit led and moving under the anointing and simply allowing God to take control.

Chapter Eight
God Wants His Church Back

So many small churches are not going anywhere. They have no vision. The pastors just have a maintenance ministry, preaching much of the same stuff over and over again to the same little group of people hoping that they will get their revelation. They don't see that without a vision the people perish. *"Where there is no vision the people perish . . ."* (Prov.29:18).

True spiritual revelation will create a hunger in people when they see that there is so much more that God has to offer them. If they are ignorant of **full** salvation, then it's like nibbling on the appetizers or hors d'œuvres, rather than enjoying the banquet. Also it's not enough to say there is a banquet, but we have to serve it. And that is what was happening then and still is today, if you know where to go. Other churches are *'seeking'* churches that say they are looking for God or more of Him. *"Open my eyes Lord that I might see Jesus."* is a one of the songs that they sing. Personally I would prefer to join a *'finding'* church rather than a *'seeking'* one. While they are seeking and looking and asking and pleading, it means they haven't received Him and all that He has purchased for them yet, or maybe they have only tasted that little snack or appetizer. "We have been seeking and searching after God for twenty years. Come and join us in the search." "Thanks very much, but that doesn't appeal to me."

There was, and still is, so much that we do in church which is **not** based on New Testament concepts. We discovered God had ideas of His own about how to do things. The main earthquake among us was the discovery that God's Spirit wanted to use everyone. The old people, the young people, the middle-aged people, the youth, the children, the banker, the trash man, the clerk, the housewife, the plumber etc. The anointing, we found out was for everyone. God just took over; we really didn't know how to "have a meeting"(or as some would say) "how to have church," so we had to depend on God. We didn't just want a **good** meeting, we wanted a **God** meeting. The Holy Spirit began to teach us how to listen and "tune in" to what He was saying.

God used everyone. We didn't have a front, we didn't have a pulpit, we didn't have a platform we didn't have a worship team to lead us into the presence of God. We came into the presence of God and when we met it was like an explosion of life. The Bible says, "When you come together brothers and sisters **everyone** of you, has a song, a tongue, an interpretation, a prophecy etc. It was like an orchestra with all the various instruments and the Great Conductor who touches the instruments and plays a beautiful melody. That's what happens when we truly allow God's Spirit to direct us.

We learned to listen to the Holy Spirit and give what He gave to us. There was no form or pattern of service. The Holy

Spirit gave us songs, and prophetic words, and visions, and tongues and interpretations and teachings and encouragements and words of knowledge. As people were led by the Holy Spirit a wonderful melody was created. All the instruments moved together under the conductor to create a marvelous tune. If someone started out a song or gave a word which was contrary to what the Spirit of God was saying, it would die on their lips.

The people became so tuned in and mature enough to the Spirit of God that they did not join in or respond to the opposite of what the Spirit of God was saying; so even good songs and good words were not necessarily received, because the people wanted God's words and songs for the meeting. I remember at South Chard when a famous international Bible teacher stood up to teach, but sat down a few minutes later, because his teaching wasn't in tune with what the Spirit of God was saying.

Needs were met as people met with God. At the end of the meeting no one had any doubt what God had said to us in that meeting. And Oh yes, the musicians sat among the people. Sometimes the Lord gave one of the musicians a song for us all to sing and sometimes maybe a prophesy in song or one of the instruments would come under the anointing, but it was all part of the message God was bringing forth and speaking to us at that time. The "proceeding" word was released. The musicians didn't come to church with a pre-selected list of songs, as we never knew what the Holy Spirit might do or say. Sometimes the Lord gave a song to a child and the musicians would pick it up and play and sing with the child, and it would often turn out to be the "Word of the Lord for that situation. God gave many people songs and they would begin to sing. The musicians would simply put into the right key and pick it up so that we could all join in.

Stephen a young lad of about twelve stood up one Sunday morning in the middle of the meeting. He placed his Bible upon the floor and stood on it because he had read something about "standing on the Word." He placed a handkerchief on his head (not sure what that was about) and sang a few lines from a song; "I will bless the Lord at all times; His praise shall continuously be in my mouth." Before we knew it, a wind rushed into the building and knocked a hundred saints on the floor and that was the end of that meeting!

One Sunday morning Chris, a young evangelist who often traveled with me, stood up in a crowded meeting with many visitors and said, "There are six people here that are involved in immorality and if they don't stand up and acknowledge it, I will stand in front of you one by one until you do." It didn't take more than a few seconds before six people arose for confession and prayer. Young teenagers from an evangelical church said that they were scared when they visited our fellowship. In their own church they could mess about at the back and sneak out and mess around with the boys in the parking lot during the service, but here anything could happen and their sins could be exposed.

Another time an Anglican pastor visited our Thursday evening meeting. It was a wonderful meeting and the Holy Spirit flowed through many members. After the meeting was over the pastor came to me and commented on how wonderful the meeting was. He then asked how long did we practice and rehearse to have such a successful meeting. When I told him we just came together and depended on the Holy Spirit, not knowing what was going to happen, he was amazed, he couldn't believe it.

Most charismatic churches today have a three part format; a time of praise and worship which can last anything from 30 minutes to 90 minutes; then 45 minutes of preaching and about 40 minutes of ministry. It reminds of my grandson's eating habits. If he has meat, peas and potatoes he separates them and he will first eat the peas, then the potatoes and finally the meat. It seems very strange to me to eat like that as I like to mix my food and have some of each. I find eating the same food for too long becomes monotonous and boring. It's the same with the traditional meeting format it becomes boring, because only when you allow the Holy Spirit to take over the meeting it becomes spontaneous and exciting.

So our whole meetings were all worship, (but not led by a bunch of worship leaders) but by the Holy Spirit so that songs were spirit led which was intermingled with prophecies, visions, revelations, teachings, offerings, singing scripture and singing and worshiping in the spirit and anyone (including children) could be used.

Jesus said in Matt. 4 *"Man shall not live by bread alone but by every word that PROCEEDS from the mouth of God."* We live by the proceeding word that comes from the throne: What is God saying to us TODAY? That is the proceeding word. That is the word that imparts life and faith to move us to the next thing that God has for us.

We truly believe that a lot of leaders quench out the move of the Spirit and shut it down because they don't know the Holy Spirit well enough to allow Him to take over. That's a shame because it is beautiful to see God use everyone. In the meetings God often uses the kids to demonstrate His power. This shows that you don't have to have a special qualification for God to use you; for He will use whoever is willing and available. Remember there is no age in the spirit.

When worship is spirit led, it is always scriptural. All the songs connect, because they follow a divine pattern and have a theme. They are initiated in heaven. God has something to say and to show us and when we respond accordingly in our worship, preaching, teaching, sharing and spiritual gifts, the whole Body is edified and we end up knowing that we met with God and not merely with each other. God will be in your midst and you will know it. He speaks to us through the songs sung, the message or messages, prophesies, visions, words given and the testimonies shared. They all fit together and complement each other, so every joint is supplied. (Col.2:19. Eph 4:16.)

It also affects everyone of every age. We gather together, not merely for singing, teaching and prayer, but for Celebration, Exhortation and Revelation. We are to exhort one another, each of you have a song, a revelation, a teaching, etc. When it's done in order (not a programmed order of service, but God's order) it fits together and gives us revelation and empowers and inspires our spirits. When we come together, come in faith expecting supernatural happenings, expecting the angels to come and worship with us and encourage us. Expect the miraculous, expect His love to abound and most of all expect to receive glimpses of His Glory. Let God get glory in the church both now and evermore! God wants His church back!

Chapter Nine
Small Miracles That Were Great

We were being thrown into the deep end by the ministers visiting us from the church at Chard. If someone needed deliverance, or Baptism, or be filled with the Spirit, they told **us** to do it. I remember being told to minister to this man that had just come back from the mission field. I had only been in this new realm a few days. He had been a missionary for forty years and was well known in his field. He was dry and depressed by negative spirits. I ministered to him and was amazed to see him totally transformed by the power of God. I didn't have a degree in counseling, but neither did Jesus. We got to know a Christian clinical Psychiatrist who was the top man at a London teaching hospital. From time to time he would send people to us for deliverance, as he was unable to perform deliverance at his hospital.

There were so many people hungry that we were invited to many places. One time we went to Lady Astor's stately home where Catholic Priests and students were attending Charismatic meetings. I remember preaching to them and seeing many of them falling on their knees; coming under conviction. Another time the actor friend, Timmy invited some of the school girls from a private school where his daughter went to come to a meeting to hear me preach at a medical doctor's house who was the brother in law of the Clinical Psychiatrist we mentioned. Two famous British stage and movie stars, John Mills and Richard Attenborough lived nearby on Richmond Green and some of their children went to that school. About fifteen girls came to the actor's house for the meeting, including Richard Attenborough's twelve year old daughter. Almost all the girls received salvation and the baptism of the Spirit. They ended up jumping around like bunnies praising the Lord and speaking in tongues. Unfortunately it didn't go down well with the two famous actors when they found out, for they forbade their children to come back again.

The students at the local art college were coming to our meetings and bringing their friends. One teenage boy with a guitar was brought to our house for ministry whose father was either a Baptist pastor or a Methodist minister. The boy was hungry for more of God and after prayer was filled with the Spirit. His name was Graham Kendrick who later became a top Christian song writer and artist.

Because of what was happening in our fellowship we were invited to minister in different places. Also many school kids were coming to our meetings and the public schools had opened the doors to us. We started going into the local schools with guitars and songs. We preached to the kids and hundreds began to come to the Lord. Often we would give out words of knowledge and the skeptics would be silenced. Most schools had a 'Christian Union.' A small group of five or six Christians would meet once a week during lunch hour for prayer and Bible study. We would come in as guest speakers and they would advertise. Very soon the 'Christian Unions' would grow to the hundreds as revival broke out in the schools. When the head boy or head girl in the school accepted Christ it had a tremendous impact on the other students.

Because of this revival in the schools, we started "Youth Ministries" on Friday night at the market hall. Busloads of kids came to the meetings and we arranged for Christian singers and musicians to perform and share. There was the British pair Malcolm & Alwen; also many came from the States, such as Chuck Girard, Bob Cull, Larry Norman, Randy Matthews and Jamie Owens the daughter of Jimmy and Carol Owens, the popular American Christian songwriters and authors.

Jamie stayed with us and came several times and on her last visit she was very enthusiastic in telling us of a different kind of church in California which she had joined called, "The Vineyard," which appeared to have been the first or one of the first churches that John Wimber had started.

Donnie a young lad played Spanish guitar. One evening I had him play for the youth. They thought he would strum his guitar, sing and play some choruses, so when he exercised his fingers before playing they thought he was messing around, but as soon as he started to play they were all mesmerized and he brought the house down.

In our town, we ministered in the streets to the young people. We also had street meetings. The first open air meeting we had was outside in the same place that we worshiped on Sunday morning in the market hall. The Lord challenged us by asking if we were willing to be free in the open air as we were in the meetings and not be self-conscious or embarrassed. It was a challenge, so the first time we had the open air meeting was more for us than for the onlookers. We drew quite a crowd and as we worshiped with our guitars and danced before the Lord, others would go around and witness to the spectators. We were learning more and more to become Christ conscious rather than man or self-conscious.

One day Kathie was walking along the high street with her shopping bag and was singing praises softly to herself as she walked along. The Lord challenged her as He did to us all a short time before. "You praise Me loudly and lift your hands up in the meeting."

She agreed.

Then God said, "Why don't you do that now?"

She replied, "But I'm by myself."

Then the Lord said, "You don't want another religious spirit that I delivered you from, do you?"

She replied "No Lord, I don't. I already got delivered from about six."

The Lord said, "You have to be the same here as in the meeting."

Note: English high streets are often as busy as American malls at Christmas so they were people everywhere. She thought, "Well, OK" and she put her bag over her shoulder and raised her hand up and closed her eyes so she wouldn't see people watching her. She didn't want to witness the horrified look on their faces by making a spectacle of herself. Remember this is England and people didn't do that kind of thing back then. She sang as loudly as she could and kept her arm up in the air. After a minute or so she opened her eyes and people were staring at her with unbelief. Because she felt embarrassed, she lifted her arm and pretended she was waving to a friend from across the street. Then she felt bad so she decided to go for it. So she closed her eyes, raised both her hands in the air and walked along with her eyes closed singing as loud as she could. After a while she came around and found herself clinging to a lamppost, totally drunk in the spirit and surrounded by a crowd that were laughing with her, but not at her, as Holy Ghost laughter is infectious. She was able to hand out some tracts and witness to some folks.

Another time Kathie was walking home from being with a friend. Suddenly a man jumped out from a hedge as she passed this house. He said, *"I've been watching you. What's that on you?"*

She jumped back and replied, *"Oh! It must be Jesus."*

"Well my brother is a Jehovah's Witness and he doesn't have that."

Kathie replied, *"I can tell you where I live,"* thinking he might come to our house meeting.

He snapped back, *"We all know where you live!"* confirming that he and others had been watching us and then walked off.

Our young people would also go and stand outside the local pubs and witness to everyone. Some of the customers were too scared to come out and others were too scared to go in when we were there. They would warn everyone that the *'Jesus Freaks'* are back in town. Andy, one of the students, got saved outside the pub and his life was so transformed that he took a bunch of records and record equipment that he had stolen from the stores to the police station and asked if he could take it back. He had to go to court, but the judge did pardon him from going to jail, as he saw his transformed life and his willingness to do restitution. He then became very active in the fellowship.

Another boy who was saved which is worth mentioning was the leader of the "Hells Angels." He was concerned that he might be in danger and we had to help him to stay safe for a while. During that period we didn't turn on the TV for about six months, not because we thought it was sinful, but we were so caught up with what God was doing and so much was going on we never had the time. The wonderful thing was that it was not some kind of religious endeavor, but we were carried along by the spirit.

One time we went into a Methodist Youth club and preached to the kids there. They turned off the music, stopped playing pool and table tennis, and flocked around us. They were so hungry to learn about God and Jesus. As the club was closing they asked us if we could return tomorrow and tell them more. The leader of the youth group was furious as we had spoiled his evening. He said he did not want us to return and the youth were very disappointed; so here was an unbelieving Methodist youth leader forbidding the kids hearing the Gospel.

We then began to receive invitations from fellowships in other parts of the country. We would have meetings at their homes or churches and then go into the local schools, colleges and universities. We frequently visited a fellowship in Portsmouth, a Naval town on the south coast of England. One of the young people who came to the meetings was a hippie with long hair who worked as a gardener in the public parks. He and his wife and their two babies sat in all our meetings. They would put the babies under the chairs where they would sleep during the long meetings. That young hippie eventually became well known as a prophet and now lives and ministers in the USA. His name is Graham Cooke.

While we were traveling and ministering around the country, meetings were still going on in our home. We remember returning to our house during a meeting. Somebody we had never seen before opened the door and welcomed us into the meeting. We asked him where he was from and he said he was staying at our house as he had been in a meeting in Chard and he was looking for a fellowship and somewhere to stay and they had said he could stay here. Later when we moved into the hall at the town center; when we returned and went to the meeting, greeters would come up and welcome us to the fellowship and asked if we had been here before and we had only been away a couple of weeks. They were telling us how wonderful the meetings were, they knew about us, but at that point they had never seen us.

Many people were coming; especially students. We had been so bound up in doctrine with no life that we had to be free. The Holy Spirit fell on us and for a long season we continued with laughter. Tears would flow as we would helplessly sink on the floor and laugh. After many weeks of this we began to feel that we should experience a godly sorrow. We began to feel guilty for enjoying ourselves so much. So we cried out to God to show us our sins so that we could weep for them. Instead of that happening the laughter increased tenfold. When Richard, who was African, first came to the meeting he was very suspicious as different rumors about our meetings were circulating in the area. After the meeting started and we were praising the Lord, I will never forget seeing Richard slide down the wall with a big grin and his head shaking as the tears of joy run down his round black face.

One of our Christian brothers Brian worked at the London School of Music, which was next door to the famous Albert Hall in Kensington London. He opened the door for me to come and preach at their Christian union. I remember a female student asking me where I was from. When I told her she asked, *"Oh!*

Have you heard of a sect that meet in a house where this man who calls himself a priest and his wife who calls herself a priestess, baptized people three times in an old tin bath?"

I knew she was talking about us, but because it was so distorted I answered correctly. *"No, I have never heard of them. I didn't know there was such a group in our area."* Anyway I did continue to preach to those music students quite regularly.

I corresponded with Dr. Martyn Lloyd Jones when he had made some comments about the healing ministry of Katherine Kuhlman. He had visited America and had seen her on TV. He said that she seemed to be Christian and preached the gospel, but he wasn't sure of her doctrine. I tried to explain that she had a very emotional and moving experience with the Lord and he had more of an academic doctrinal approach to Christianity. Not everyone is the same. That's when he wrote back and told me he believed in miracles and the gifts. He even mentioned how a person was raised from the dead through the prayers of a 17th century reformer. A few months later he was a guest speaker at a local Baptist church so I went to hear him and had the opportunity of talking to him after the service. I told him some of my testimony and what happened to me. He was very thrilled. I will never forget what he said to me, *"I believe in the Holy Spirit. "I believe in the 'Corinthian church.' I believe in the gifts of the spirit. Mind you! All things should be done decently and in order. But Go on! Go on!"*

Years later, I read his biography where he had said he regretted that Westminster Chapel was only a teaching center and he didn't have a Corinthian Church which was the New Testament pattern.

Mac and Pauline, a young married couple were part of the Antioch and attended Westminster Chapel. Mac had been raised in the Brethren Assembly from a small child. Whenever we wanted to know where a certain scripture was, we asked Mac and he always knew where it could be found. After we were filled with the spirit, Pauline really received and Mac kind of followed, but seemed to be lacking something. We even paid for him to go to a Kathryn Kuhlman meeting in California because he wanted to see or experience a miracle, but although he saw many miracles he received nothing personally.

They both had a little girl and later Pauline had her second pregnancy, but after a while she began to have complications. Ian came and prayed for her, but sadly she lost her pregnancy. A few months later Pauline became pregnant again. The same problem arose and she called Ian, but he was out of the area so he called and asked us to pray for her. He said, "Don't pray for healing for I believe she has a spirit of infirmity and it needs to be cast out." We went over to their house and they both sat on their couch and we prayed and cast that spirit out of Pauline. She didn't make any kind of noise, but she began to shake violently and her eyes started to roll from side to side and then to the back of her head. Within a few minutes she was delivered; the complications ceased and she continued to have a perfect pregnancy. After we had prayed for Pauline, Kathie felt we should pray for Mac as well. As she began to pray she had a vision of a typewriter. There were words typed on the paper in the typewriter which read, *"Love you."* The words were very formal and not personal. He couldn't say to Jesus, *"I love you,"* it was too personal for him. We cast a religious spirit out of Mac and he was set free from the religious spirit, but unfortunately he never received true salvation or the baptism of the Holy Spirit. For all those years of faithful church going, daily Bible reading and studying he had been operating in a religious spirit. Now that had gone sadly he had no interest in spiritual matters and he became worldly.

Bernard was a dark skinned young man who came from Persia. He was very religious and kept the rules of his religion for years, but was frustrated because he wanted to know God. He finally prayed a prayer and said unless God revealed Himself within three days he would throw in the towel and never pray or believe again. Two days later, one of the students at the local college brought him to one of our meetings and that's where his prayer was answered. Bernard faithfully became part of the fellowship and met and then married Kirsty, a blue eye blonde girl from Finland who was a student at Loughboro or Leicester University in the Midlands who was saved during the time when we were preaching there. She then moved down to be with us after she came to the Lord and that's how she met Bernard.

Many of the students were hungry for the spirit, but sometimes did bizarre things. Many traditional believers from historic dominations would say, *"There you are leading these poor ignorant kids astray filling their minds with all this weird super spiritual stuff like speaking in tongues, visions, healing and prophecies, that's all finished, we only need the scriptures now."*

But they were learning to walk in a new realm, just like a child learns to walk and falls several times. God has put in our hearts a hunger for His divine nature which is more than just believing in a book, even if it is the Bible. Many traditional, orthodox, church leaders worship the Bible, but only have a religious life rather than a supernatural life. When we were at the Antioch I ministered to one of Angela's friends whose name was June; a shapely blonde bombshell who was in the entertainment business as a pinup girl. She said, *"I've always had a Bible and I put it next to my bed every night and before I go to sleep I kiss it for protection."*

I asked her, *"Have you ever opened it and read it?"*

She answered, *"No."*

We led her to the Lord and she turned many men's heads when she walked down the isle at Westminster Chapel. When we saw her sometime later, she was no longer a blonde bombshell, but she now had brown hair and was working for the Billy Graham Organization.

In the revival, we were working with a lot of newly saved or young churchy college students who were not instructed well in the scriptures. Many of them were immature. I remember one young girl that brought this boy to us called Karl. He was wild looking and wore a turtle neck sweater. The strange thing was that he had the collar up so high that it was just below his eyes. His hair was all over the place. We decided he needed deliverance. We asked him if he was saved and he replied that he was saved and was washed in the blood of the Holy Ghost. By then we knew that he wasn't right and needed deliverance. As we prayed he was becoming more agitated. After the first session I asked the young girl about Karl and she said that God told her to marry him. I then said that I didn't think he was fit for marriage in the state he was in and did she love him. She said no, but God told her he was to be her cross to bear. Fortunately, I was able to show her that God doesn't use marriage to punish her. She took him to Chard and I don't recall what became of him, except she didn't marry him.

One young student who had recently found the Lord and was coming to the fellowship arrived at our house one evening at about 9.00 pm. He was really excited. *"Praise God!"* he said, *"I was at my lodgings and felt the Lord told me to go and visit Frank and Anita, but they weren't home. Then I felt the Lord tell me to go and see Jim and Margaret, but they weren't home either, so then the Lord told me to come and visit you. It's wonderful being led by the Spirit."*

Needless to say, we had to work on him a little on how to walk in the Spirit.

Stuart was living with us for a while. We had a lot of people coming to our house and our carpet had seen better days. One day Stuart came in all excited and said, *"The Lord has told me to order you a new carpet."*

"Great! Then we will pick one out," I replied.

"I didn't know that you could afford to buy us a carpet," said Kathie.

"I can't, but I believe the Lord will give you the money to pay for it," replied Stuart.

*"If you can believe the Lord will give **us** the money to pay for it, then you should be able to believe the Lord to give **you** the money to pay for it. You ordered it, you pay!"* I replied. We did eventually get a new carpet, but not from Stuart.

Frank and Anita were with us at the Antioch and they were both filled with the spirit after Ian had prayed for them. Frank was a dreamy artistic guy, who really loved the Lord and was diligent in learning how to hear the voice of God and live in the Spirit. Frank was learning to walk in the spirit. One cold foggy winter evening he felt that the Lord had told him to make some sandwiches and a flask of hot coffee and go down by the river and minister to the street people who slept under the bridge. He arrived there around 9.00 PM and he sat down on a bench and waited.

It was becoming very cold and damp and no one was showing up. Frank waited till 11.30 PM and nobody showed. It was even too cold for the street people. So Frank ate the sandwiches drank the coffee and then he went home. What happened? It appeared he missed God, but he was learning.

One Friday evening, Kathie and I had done our grocery

shopping and finally went to bed at about 11.30 PM. We woke at 1.00 am to the sound of the door bell. Who could be at our door at this time? I went down and opened the door and Frank was standing there holding a brown paper bag with a big smile on his face. *"Frank, what are you doing here,"* I asked.

"I was praying this evening and I felt the Lord told me to come and bring you this," he replied holding the bag.

"Who is it?" Kathie called from upstairs.

"It's Frank! He said the Lord sent him," I replied.

Kathie came down and we invited Frank in. My mind began turning over thinking, what is it that he has brought us at this time of the morning? Perhaps it's the family jewels it must be something really important. Frank opened up the bag and brought out a pack of butter and 2lb bag of sugar and placed it on our coffee table with a big smile.

I began to feel angry for I was thinking, *"stupid idiot!"*

"We have been grocery shopping earlier and we have plenty of butter and sugar and even if we didn't, he could have waited until daylight or breakfast time."

I was just about to give him a piece of my mind when Kathie did what most English ladies do when there's a crises. She said, *"Well let's have a cup of tea."*

So we drank our tea, had some prayer, and said goodbye to Frank as he got on his bicycle and rode seven miles back to his house. As we climbed back up the stairs to bed I asked the Lord what was all that about?

Two things the Lord said to me.

1.   I want to teach Frank obedience.

2.   I want to teach you to grow in grace.

But that was not the end of the encounter. I needed to buy a suit so I went and out and found one that I liked, but didn't have the money to pay for it. The pants needed shortening slightly so I put a deposit down and said I would collect it in a few days. Now I needed to trust God to provide. Prior to this, we had met a young Salvation Army couple who we hungry for the things of the Spirit and were fascinated in the way that we lived. One time they were at our house and Kathie was sharing with them the life of faith. I had just returned from one of the four house meetings we had during the week. When I came through the door they asked me, *"Do you have the money for the suit yet?"*

I replied, *"No! Not yet!"* Then suddenly faith rose up in me and I said, *"Yes! I do have the money!"* and right at that moment the doorbell rang. I opened the door and who do you think was standing there? No! It wasn't Frank it was Timmy who had just returned from one of the other house meetings. He was on his way home and lived a couple of streets away. He had sold his old house in Barnes and moved to be closer to the fellowship. He said that Frank had given him an envelope to give to me. When I opened the envelope inside was the exact money for the suit, much to the amazement of the Salvation Army couple. Frank was on the way to hearing from the Lord.

Kathie invited a young Pentecostal pastor and his wife over

for dinner. They were hungry and interested in what God was doing in our fellowship. Kathie had made spaghetti and as she was dishing out the pasta she suddenly realized that she forgotten to make any spaghetti sauce. *"Oh Lord!"* she cried, *"Help me!"* She was thinking here was this pastor and his wife who were looking to us for spiritual wisdom and what on earth would they think of her. It was most embarrassing. Exactly at that moment the door bell rang I answered the door and there was Frank standing there with a larger casserole dish in his hands. *"Anita was in the kitchen and suddenly felt to make you this,"* He was carrying a dish of spaghetti sauce.

In America you hear of miracles and usually they are what are considered great ones. Tremendous healings, hundred of thousands coming to the Lord, provisions of great finances to built great temples for the Glory of God. Preachers will stand up and say, I needed a million dollars by Thursday and the Lord told me to give my last $5,000.00 away on Wednesday night and by Thursday the money came in. If you give sacrificially now in my meeting God will do the same for you. But I began to see how God did great miracles in small simple situations and how personal His blessings were. This is not necessarily seeing people do great things and becoming spiritual superstars, so one can feed off of their success, but God using our faith to bring us to a higher level to walk in the supernatural in our everyday life; even a thing as simple as providing a bowl of spaghetti sauce.

Another time Kathie and I remember going up to Bill and

Carol's house in Liverpool to minister to a bunch of young hippies that had been coming to their meetings. Bill and Carol had been touched by the revival and were ministering to many young people in their area. There were about twelve to fifteen of them at their house and they all looked a mess. I remember when the meetings started and they were singing a well known hymn. A number of them were standing with a hymn book in one hand and a lighted cigarette in the other. As they sang, *"Long my imprisoned spirit lay, fast bound in sin and natures night; Thine eye diffused a quickening ray, I awoke, the dungeon flamed with light. My chains fell off, my heart was free, I rose, went forth and followed thee."* and took a big drag on their weed. We couldn't believe it. Then the Holy Spirit said to us, "Say nothing, just love and accept them. I will set them free." As we preached revelation and truth to them they opened their hearts to all that God had for them and in a day or so they discarded their smokes and many negative worldly practices without us having to say a word or point out the things that were contrary to God's best. Even the girls changed their appearances and began to wear nice dresses and look pretty, instead of looking like Rachael Ragamuffin.

As more people were coming to the Lord, Bill and Carol started using the new converts to reach their friends. On Saturday mornings they would dress down in casual clothes and go out and witness. One Saturday morning they arranged to meet outside a bank. One of the boys that showed up was wearing a dog collar. Bill was amazed and asked, *"Why are you wearing a dog collar? You're not a vicar."*

"I thought it would be a help when preaching to the kids." he replied.

"Well, if you want to come with us you need to remove that collar," said Bill.

The young man refused to remove his collar so they decided to leave him outside the bank. Then he lay down in the street and said he wouldn't move unless he could come with his dog collar, so they called his bluff and left. After some time, Bill went back to see what he was doing. When he arrived a small crowd had gathered. When he asked what was going on they told him that this poor vicar had collapsed outside the bank so they sent for an ambulance and he was taken to the hospital. So Bill and a couple of the others went over to the hospital and found him lying on a bed. The doctors had been examining him, but couldn't figure out what was wrong with him. They went to him and told him to get up, but he refused; they told him again to get up and then he said,

"Only if you lay hands on me and pray for me."

They replied, *"You must be kidding, now get up!"*

But again he refused, so they finally laid hands on him and prayed for him to rise in the name of Jesus. He immediately rose up and walked out of the hospital, much to the amazement of the doctors. Even in this great revival there still some people doing strange and stupid things. Yet on reflection it was very funny.

Ted was a pensioner that started coming to the meetings. He traveled quite a long distance on his auto-cycle which was less powerful than a motorbike. We don't recall how he came to be with us, but he was pretty harmless although he seemed to like the girls. I think he was a lonely soul and enjoyed being with us. When he arrived at the meetings he would take off his helmet and his waterproof oilskins which he wore and then he would methodically with a great rustling noise put his belongings into little bags.

Timmy would always greet people with a Holy kiss, a hug, and say, *"Dear one."* After Ted had been coming for sometime Timmy said to me, *"I don't believe Ted is saved! He just comes for the girls or because he is lonely; he doesn't really understand about spiritual things."* Timmy had tried to talk to Ted and kept saying that these deep things about the spirit are very hard to understand. Timmy went into great detail trying to explain how completed it was. Ted's replied, *"Tim you seem a little confused."* Timmy really wanted Ted to leave the fellowship, but didn't want to offend him. Timmy said to me, *"I'm not going to hug and kiss Ted anymore when he leaves."* So that evening in our house meeting Ted was getting ready to leave. He called to Timmy and said, *"Goodbye Tim"* expecting Timmy to jump up and warmly say goodbye with a hug and kiss, but Timmy just sat on our couch with his back to Ted and shouted, *"Goodbye Ted!"* So Ted came up behind Timmy and planted a big kiss on the back of his neck. Everyone thought that was hilarious.

Duggie was a beach bum who was stoned on drugs and thought he was Jesus. When we met him he was so stoned and in such a terrible condition we couldn't talk or reason with him. His mind was completely blown. The Holy Spirit told us to sing to him. Back in those days we almost always sang scripture. As we sang to him over and over again his mind started to heal and gradually he came to his right senses and was gloriously saved. He became a very faithful believer and lived with us for a time. Sometimes he would have relapses with his mind and behaved in strange ways, but he really loved the Lord.

He was very simple and wasn't able to work in a high paid job. He did get work as a city street cleaner. He was given a wheel barrow with a broom and shovel and he would go along the streets and sweep the gutters and put the rubbish in his wheel barrow. He loved to witness to people and would ask them, *"If you died tonight, where would you go?"* On day Duggie met this girl on the bus and witnessed to her. He was learning to move in spiritual gifts. After telling her the gospel he asked if she had a hearing problem. She told him she was deaf in one ear. He asked her if he could pray for her. She said sure and thought he would pray for her when he went home, but Duggie put his hand on her ear and started praying loudly in tongues and commanding the deaf spirit to leave. He then asked her if her ear was better and she replied it was the wrong ear.

A few days later he was out with his wheel barrow and saw her across the street and so he went running across the road to pray for her again. When saw him she tried to avoid him by running across the road and was hit by a motorcycle and landed up in hospital. Duggie then tried to come to her ward at the hospital to pray for her again, until we advised him to leave well alone. Duggie kept in touch with us and in 2005 told us he was married and still serving the Lord with his wife.

When we were at the Antioch Derek recommended that we purchased a Scofield Bible. We knew he had plenty of notes to explain doctrine, but we didn't realize at that time that he was a dispensationalist. After we came into revival we discarded our Scofield Bibles. During the revival a number of young people needed deliverance and George was one of them. He was a kind of hippie with long hair and a beard. He was almost illiterate and had many hang-ups, but was hungry for the Lord. We started to pray for him and he began to manifest with screams and yells. As we lived in a duplex house, our Baptist neighbors were freaking out. Our door bell started to ring and Kathie went to the door and the Baptist neighbor (his face as black as thunder) said, *"What on earth is going on?"* Kathie a little taken aback replied, *"Oh we are casting our demons, but it is legal."*

The neighbor backed away with a terrified look on his face and hurriedly left. We then immediately took George down to the shed at the bottom of our back garden and again began praying and casting out the spirits. Eventually this strange voice screamed from him and began to say, *"I'm not coming out, because you haven't fasted enough."*

As we said, "*They shall cast out devils."*

The voice screamed again, *"You can't say that it's not in*

the original; Scofield said it." It was very interesting as George was obviously not well read or religious so he didn't know about Bibles or Scofield, but the demon in George knew.

I said, *"You must come out in the name of Jesus."* And that spirit did. George was transformed and became a faithful Christian.

As we were progressing and making contact with many different people we were told of an elderly couple that had been part of a sect which was led by an old grandfather of a large family. Originally there were about 40 of them that were waiting for the return of Christ. They kept changing the dates of the return when it didn't happen as prophesied. This couple lived in isolation so Kathie felt the Lord told us to go and see them. I was complaining as it was about 150 mile drive. We finally arrived at the area where they lived, but it was impossible to drive to their house. We had to walk across fields and ditches to get to them. Needless to say, I was now fussing all the more.

When we arrived they were pleased to see us and invited us in. We began to share with them how God was doing such great things and we told them about Chard which was the closest to where they lived. We encouraged them to visit that Sunday. The next thing we found out was they did go and were so impacted that they continued driving there every Sunday until they finally sold their house and moved to Chard to be with the fellowship. They said that we were used of God to bring them back into life as they had been dying spiritually. I must say I had to repent to God for fussing and not believing my wife.

Another time we were invited by Tony, a minister from Chard, to visit Ireland with him to speak at some meetings. There was also a group of American teenagers from Bob Mumford's Church with us. We had a good time, but during the last meeting we felt God told us to give all our money we had in the offering. A bunch of us from the church caught the bus to take us to the ocean ferry to England. Although we had a return ferry ticket we had no money for the bus so we got on by faith. As the ticket collector was coming towards us to take our fares we didn't know what to do except believe. Just as he approached us, one of the persons in the bus called out and said, *"David and Kathie. I got your tickets."*

We said, *"Thank you Jesus!"* But we still had to pick up our car drive 150 miles home and we didn't have enough petrol in the tank for that.

On the way back to London we had to pass near Chard so we stopped and visited three different friends. We had some nice fellowship and tea and biscuits (cookies) at the first two houses, but no gas money. We decided to visit Ian and Rosemary before we left. I remember Ian telling me that one time he was driving and was able to travel seventy miles on an empty tank by using his faith. I was wondering if I could reach to that same faith level. We had a good time with them, but nothing seemed forthcoming in my trail of faith. I didn't want to say or hint anything so the pressure mounted. As we were getting ready to leave I said that I was going ahead to the car. I walked down the long path from their front door trying to figure out how God would enable us to get home. I opened the glove compartment and found some small change and also a bunch of postage stamps and I was trying to work out if they would take the stamps and how much would I have to buy some gas. Kathie followed me down the path with Rosemary. As Kathie climbed in to the passenger seat Rosemary tapped on the window and said, *"The Lord told me to give you this"* and put twenty pounds (about $35.00) into her hand; needless to say we had more than enough to cover our need for fuel. When we arrived back at our house there was a meeting in progress, so we took great pleasure in testifying of God's wonderful provision.

In one of our house meetings we had invited a curate and his wife to come. The wife used to go to the Antioch with us before she was married. She was now the wife of a high church Anglican Curate. Her mother was one of the queen's ladies in waiting, so they were rather posh and high class, but also very hungry. We had been having wild meetings and were praying that the Lord would tone down the meeting as we didn't want to frighten them off. We had a front and back room with dividing doors which we would open up for the meetings. This made it into one nice long room. With people sitting on the stairs we sometimes crowded seventy people into our duplex. In the front of the room there was a large bay window with a window seat that could accommodate at least six people.

The meeting started and after a while Gwen a missionary who was sitting on the window seat began to shake. Then suddenly she literally flew through the air; through the opened doors, and landed on her back in the rear room. I thought, *"Great that's done it! Why did this have to happen tonight?"* The funny thing was that the curate and his wife both had their eyes closed and didn't even notice it. A little later I asked, *"Who wants to be filled with the spirit?"* Both of them immediately stood up. I said, *"Come over here and I will pray for you."* As soon as I said that they both fell to the floor and began speaking in tongues. I was a little frustrated as I was ready to pray for them and God did it without me. Later I realized how awesome He was.

Things were still happening in our local town of Kingston, not only in the local schools but out in the town and on the streets. Gerald Coates was a young mailman that ran a youth outreach and rode around on bicycle when we first met him. He was very active and we did some things together locally even though he lived in Cobham about fifteen miles out of the area. Gerald eventually became a key leader in the house church movement and gained national recognition being instrumental in leading Sir Malcolm Muggeridge to the Lord. I believe he also met the queen in later years.

In Tolworth, a town a few miles away from our local town we went to a girl's school and a boy's school. The first time I preached was to a small group of fifteen year old girls in a lunch time Christian union meeting. After I finished about eight of them were weeping and falling apart. The bell went and the teacher and other girls were returning to class. I was concerned as I wasn't sure what to do. But when the principal found out what had happened she had me preach to the whole assembly several times. (Unknown to me she was a Christian and also a doctor of divinity) A revival broke out in that school and the head girl was saved amongst many others that came to the Lord. We also went into many schools in Leicester and ministered to all the age groups.

The same thing happened at the boy's school across the road and the head boy was saved and again I preached to the whole school under the watchful eye of the headmaster. He told me I wasn't allowed to make an altar call so I said at the end of my message that I wasn't allowed to make an altar call, but if I was, this is what I would say. I then told what they had to do to get saved. After it was over the headmaster said to his students, *"If you would like to know more or speak to our speaker you can return after sign off and talk to him."* We waited in the hall as all the students went to sign off for the day and after about ten minutes the doors flew open and dozens and dozens came back in for prayer and commitment. In both of the schools the Christian union grew from around 15 to around 150.

One of the young people brought Nigel to our house to be prayed for to receive the Holy Spirit. After showing him some relevant scriptures, we sat him on a chair to pray for him to receive. After a short while he and the chair began to bounce all round the room and at the same time he was crying out, *"Bubitty! Bubitty! Bubitty!"*

I thought, that sounds a strange language for speaking in tongues. The amazing thing was his life was totally transformed in that moment. He was turned from a quiet studious kind of boy, into a bold lion. He went back to his school and revival broke out and hundreds of students came to the Lord. After he graduated he went on to Bristol University and revival broke out there. He joined a fellowship which was led by Don Morris who was the man who we first saw preach at Chard with the golden face. Nigel arranged for me come to Bristol University and preach and also at Don's fellowship.

If you recall, John who had followed me up at the Antioch, had now been filled with the Spirit and was the headmaster at public boarding school (which in the UK is a private school) in Skegness a coastal town in the north of England. When John heard what was happening to us, he invited me to come and minister to the students. I decided to take Chris the young evangelist with me. We had some good meetings but there was one young man who was a bit of a ring leader with a little following, who challenged me when I was preaching by asking a question.

"Mr. Walters!" he said. *"Wouldn't you say that all these things you preach about God, Angels and Jesus, is just make believe pie in the sky? After all, this is just a crutch and we need to be in charge of our own destiny and not depend upon religion."*

He then sat down with a smirk on his face amid a handful of his followers cheering and clapping him.

"Well you have created a problem for me." I replied.

He smiled even more with a satisfied look upon his face as his followers continued to cheer him.

"How old are you?" I asked.

"Fifteen,".

Then I replied, *"Your argument which I don't believe originated with you as I have heard it many times before is very weak, because you are asking me to believe a fifteen year old boy's opinion, against Jesus Christ who has influenced and changed the lives of millions of people though out history. Countless multitudes have been healed, delivered, and set free by believing in Him. He has had more influence on history than any other living creature. In fact, He split time in half as we are now in 1972 AD. Now I'm not a betting man, but if I had to choose between a fifteen year old schoolboy and Jesus Christ I would bet on Jesus every time."*

Then practically the whole school cheered, much to the dismay of the boy and his handful of followers.

Another time Chris and I went to a school in Tibshelf, a town in the north midlands of England. A number of youngsters were saved at the school meeting so we invited them to the vicarage where we were staying with the vicar and his family. It was a large Victorian house and we had the meeting in a large room. About twenty kids showed up and I began to teach on spiritual gifts. After a while I felt the Lord was revealing things to the children especially to one little boy. I finally said to him, *"The Lord has given you something hasn't he?"*

He said, *"Yes."*

I then asked him to share it and he said, *"No."*

He was shy, finally I persuaded and he had about three different things and one was for a child who needed healing. The child was prayed for and was instantly healed. Then a boy of about ten who had just gotten saved that day suddenly said, *"Mr. Walters! God has given me a song. Can I sing it?"*

I was obviously thrilled and said, *"Yes."*

He sang these words to a wonderful tune,

"Daddy I want you to know that I love you.

Only because You first loved me.

I want to praise You and thank You for everything,

And Glorify Your Holy name."

I took that little boy's song to America and taught it at many churches, including Jamie Buckingham's church in Melbourne Florida.

One time when Chris and I were on our travels we ministered at this old church hall in the Midlands to a bunch of teenagers. It was Chris' time to preach. As he was preaching a Deacon use the toilet which was right behind where Chris was preaching. As the Deacon went in to use the urinal, the door slowly swung open so they could see his back. The kids began to giggle and try to smother their laughter. Chris thought they were laughing at him and began to rebuke them as he was preaching a serious message. This made them laugh even more. I had to explain to Chris later what had happened.

Another time we were traveling and ministered at some place and received little or no offering so we began to pray that God would meet our needs. A friend of ours, Evangelist David Willows was holding a Glory Meeting in the next town so we decided to go. When we arrived the meeting had just started. After a while David saw us and suddenly called out. "We have David Walters visiting us this evening. Come on out brother"

I thought he was going to ask me to preach, but he said, "Let's bless our Brother. I want you to come up and put money in his pocket. He does a great work with the kids."

To my embarrassment and delight my pockets were stuffed with money and my neck was covered with hugs. God provided.

We also traveled several times to North London, Kent, Newcastle, Birmingham, Manchester Bristol, and Peterhead in the north east coast of Scotland where we had open air meetings on the ocean front with the popular Scottish singing and preaching family known as '*The Camerons.*' Philip Cameron the son of Simon Cameron was the first male in the Cameron clan for two hundred years <u>never</u> to have known the curse of alcoholism. When God began to move in the family, sixty-seven Camerons came to Christ in a short six-week period!

Chapter Ten
The Church has too many Fire-Trucks

Almost every church will say that they desire revival, but most of them are fearful of fire. Often when I preach in churches I ask the saints if they are **hungry** for revival? I then ask for a show of hands of those who **desire** revival. Apart from a few goofy teenagers and some very small children, just about everyone puts their hands up, including the leadership.

Obviously you wouldn't be popular in church if your raised your hand to say you definitely **didn't** want revival. It's the accepted and expected response to **want** revival. The trouble is that when revival happens you are immediately taken out of your comfort zone and things can go a bit wild. *"Well brother we don't want wild fire in our church; just a nice pleasant fire to warm us up a bit. Keep it in the grate and keep it controlled."*

God told John to write to the church of the Laodiceans, *"I know your works, that you are neither cold nor hot. I could wish you were cold or hot. So then, because you are lukewarm and neither cold nor hot, I will spew you out of My mouth."* (Rev.3:15-16)

True revival is not always nice, sweet and comforting. It's often quite the opposite. It has the ingredients to offend people. When the fire of God falls, religious spirits manifest, scream and eventually leave. Revival fire does two things it draws people, (everyone is drawn to watch a fire) for others it's too hot and they can't take it and leave. Revival is not given so we can have more of the same or enhance our programs or traditions, or make our own church grow, but it's to burn up the dross and get rid of faulty foundations. God wants His church back.

Hungry people will come, often they will flock to where revival is, and others who want to keep their traditions and comforts will leave. When the fire burns hot and God starts to take over and things happen outside of our boxes, often the leadership will try to control it. What usually happens is they call the fire station and have the firemen come with their fire trucks to put it out. Almost every church has plenty of fire trucks and firemen at the ready to quench the spirit. Have you even been in a church meeting where the spirit begins to move and someone shuts it down? There is always an excuse. *"It's out of order," "it's not in the program," "it's not been vetted by the elders," "we have gone past time."*

How about when the worship suddenly becomes anointed and the spirit is moving, and God manifests and says something very specific, yet the worship leader gets carried away (not by the spirit, but by him or herself)) and goes beyond the anointing and sings five more songs interlaced with exhortations and mini sermons. We are back again in the religious flesh.

Bible teacher Bob Mumford tells of a story of a woman sitting in church when the Holy Spirit hit her with a revelation. She was so overcome that she began to shake and shout out, *"Thank you Jesus! Glory to God! Halleluiah!"* Immediately an army of deacons came and removed her from the service. Bob Mumford said it was the quickest revival he had ever seen. It started and was over in two minutes. The fire was put out. We have no shortage of fireman and fire trucks in our churches today.

Arthur Burt, an old saint and a dear friend, who is still preaching and traveling at 100, tells of a story when he was in a church meeting and suddenly he gave out a message in tongues. Immediately an army of deacons came and escorted him out. The people that were listening to this story asked him, *"What did you do then?"*

He replied, *"I shouted the interpretation through the window."*

Aren't you glad that heaven isn't deacon possessed?

Arthur first came to our house meeting when we were traveling and we heard about it after we returned. At that time we knew about him, but we had never met. He just turned up at the meeting and sat down on the sofa with everyone else and suddenly gave out a tongue in a loud voice. He scared a young girl who was sitting next to him and as she was not used to that, she burst into tears, but he gave a wonderful message. That's what we were told, so we couldn't wait for him to come when we were home. The next time he showed up he shared so much wisdom and wonderful revelation. Arthur's main theme has always been, "Living in measure versus living in fullness" Arthur never came by invitation and you couldn't book him, he just showed up as the Spirit led him. He says, *"If your house is on fire or you have an emergency and you call the fire station, or police and ask them to come, they don't look in their appointment book and say, 'How about Wednesday week at 10.00 am. I think we can fit you in.'"*

Arthur has many stories; one more is worth telling. He was traveling on a bus and it was driving through a very open country area, when he felt the Lord told him to get off at the next stop, but it was pouring with rain. His mind said, *"That's stupid, that can't be God." "Get off at the next stop,"* said the voice again.

His mind again replied, *"That's the devil talking to you, there is no sense in getting off of the bus in the middle of nowhere in the pouring rain."*

Arthur jumped up and rang the bell and the bus pulled up at the next stop. Arthur got off of the bus and it pulled away, leaving him standing in the pouring rain without an umbrella.

A voice in his mind said, *"Idiot! Now what are you going to do?"*

Arthur then explained he was having a battle with the fanatic in the attic and the fellow in the cellar. He was the soul in the middle. The fellow in the cellar was his human reasoning and the fanatic in the attic was his spirit man. The fellow in the cellar (or basement) couldn't see as he was in the dark. The fanatic in the attic could see way up in the heavenlies. So he had to make a choice which one he would believe. Well, he had already made it. Two minutes later a car drove by; then it suddenly stopped and reversed back to where he was standing. A door flew open and a voice cried, *"Brother Arthur what are you doing here? We are just going to a meeting and the speaker couldn't make it, we need you to speak."* With that he jumped into the car, squeezed between three people and they took off.

How many of us leaders trust the Holy Spirit to have complete control? There are many leaders unfortunately who do not know the Holy Spirit well enough to trust Him to take control. How many of us are content with a good meeting rather than a God meeting? How many of us have the Fire Trucks ready and at hand as a safety measure? *"All things should be done decently and in order,"* we say.

Often we **so** emphasize **decently** and in **order** that nothing is ever allowed to be **done** unless it's by those who are deemed qualified. It's almost like the old Victorian saying, *"children should be seen and not heard."*

The main purpose of church leadership is to equip the saints that they may **do** (not sit and be spoon fed) the work of the ministry. *"And He Himself gave some to be apostles, some prophets, some evangelists, and some pastors and teachers, for the equipping of the saints for the work of the ministry, for the edifying of the body of Christ."* (Eph.4:11-12) Those five-fold ministry gifts were **not** created by God to become religious superstars that people follow and idolize.

The first time we went to a Glory revival meeting where the Camerons were saved, we were amazed to see everyone dancing. One little old man danced around us and said to Timmy who was with us at the time and was somewhat reserved, *"Brother Tim! Thirteen years ago, God touched me and set my feet a dancing and I have been dancing ever since! Halleluiah!"*

Another time during one of the glory meetings a religious minister carrying a big black Bible was present. Brother Henry, who was leading the meeting, saw him and said, *"Brother you're a minister, come up to the platform."* The minister came up with his Bible ready looking forward to preaching. Brother Henry took his Bible put it down, grabbed hold of the minister's hands and said, *"Have you ever jumped for Jesus?* Henry then jumped with the preacher all over the platform. The poor preacher lost all his pride and dignity, but found what he was really missing which was the joy and fire of the Lord and freedom of the spirit. And praise God! There were no fire trucks at those meetings.

When God takes over, will people miss it and make mistakes? Yes! We are all learning to hear from God. Will we get it right all the time? No, we won't. So what do you do if someone makes a mistake and misses it? Love them and carry on listening to the Holy Spirit.

I remember in one meeting at Chard a man started to minister a word. It was an OK scripture, but it didn't go with what

God was doing in that particular meeting. We wondered how to bring the meeting back on the God track! Suddenly the pastor's wife, known as Auntie Mill, called out at the back to the man who speaking, *"Brother, do you know that song, 'I love that man from Galilee?'"*

He shook his head and Auntie Mill said, *"Well we'll sing it."* and she proceeded to sing the song, everyone joined in and the meeting went back on the God track. The Holy Spirit knows how to deal with things without the fire trucks that quench the Spirit.

Chapter Eleven
God Does Extraordinary Things

We were off to a meeting at one school when we saw two girls outside the principal's office. There were three of us with two guitars. When they saw us and the guitars, they asked us what we were doing and where were we going? We told them we were having a meeting and invited them to join us. So they abandoned their appointment and followed us to the meeting. The Baptist teacher who was hosting the meeting seemed alarmed when she saw the girls.

"Oh dear!" she whispered, "These are the two worst girls in the school, they will ruin the meeting."

"Don't worry," we replied, *"The Lord will take care of them."* And He certainly did! When the meeting finished both of them were the first to give their hearts to the Lord.

At another school we went to, one of the kids asked,

"Are you going to ask us for money?"

"No of course not." I replied

Another then asked, *"How do you do this without getting paid then?"*

I relied, *"We have a very rich Father."*

"Wow I wish my Dad was rich!" cried another child.

We were then able to take advantage of that conversation and preach the Gospel; also telling them that our heavenly Father owned the cattle on a thousand hills and all the gold and silver belonged to Him.

We did several conferences on the Isle of Wight (a small island off the coast of the south of England) with the Portsmouth Fellowship. We met at a small Christian hotel and chapel which was run by Alistair and his wife Margaret. They were Plymouth Brethren, a small Christian sect, but now they had been filled with the spirit and were free from a lot of the religious rules which they had been governed by. There were about forty of us which included adults, teens and children.

On the Sunday evening we had finished the meeting in the chapel and went back to the house for tea, coffee and snacks. About fifteen teens asked if they could stay in the chapel and pray. About twenty minutes later after the children were given drinks and snacks and sent to bed, one of the teens called and said, *"David and Kathie come quick!"* We followed the boy back into the chapel to see an amazing sight. This sixteen year old boy who was a Catholic and was educated by monks (he had accepted the Lord during the weekend) was standing in a trance in the middle of the room surrounded by a circle of the rest of the teens.

He had his eyes closed and his hand was stretched out with his finger pointing at the teens. At the same time he was slowly moving around like the hands on a clock and each time he pointed to one of the teens, they fell to the floor and received their deliverance. It was as if the finger of God was flowing from his hands. Some of them were screaming and were trying to run away, but they couldn't because their feet were stuck to the floor.

We watched in amazement and had the wisdom not to interfere and just let it continue. We went back into the house to tell the adults what was happening and as we did suddenly an awesome presence began to manifest. Several said they heard a noise which sounded like a train. I remember that everyone stood there and like slow motion people began to put their cups of tea and coffee down as the presence engulfed them. People began to cry and shake and confess sins. This lasted about twenty minutes and suddenly we heard screaming from upstairs and all the children came rushing down crying and shaking. God had visited them as well.

Many lives were transformed that wonderful weekend and it all started by God using a brand new Christian teenager. I wonder how many pastors today could accept that a move of God came through one that wouldn't be considered to be qualified.

During this period there were large gatherings in London such as the *'Festival of Light.'* Literally thousands were gathering together and marching through the streets from many denominations and thousands of churches. We all congregated in Trafalgar square for communion. Arthur Blessitt shared and then they handed out large loaves so people could break a piece off and take communion. It was funny as one particular person in the crowd was a homeless man. When a loaf reached him he tucked it under his arm and took off running. We all finally prayed that God would bless him.

During one of the marches Timmy the actor suddenly saw another actor and his wife marching with a group. He was amazed because he knew this person was always apposed to the gospel as he had tried many times to witness him. He waved at the guy and he said he would phone him as he was curious to find out what happened. Sometime later Timmy called and this is what they told him.

They had a cat which they adored, but it became sick. They took it to the vet and after examining it he told them it had leukemia. He said they needed to have the cat put down. They were devastated and couldn't bring themselves to do that. Back at home they desperately searched through the yellow pages looking for anything listed under 'healing.' They finally came across 'The London Healing Mission.' They didn't know that particular organization really ministered to homeless people and didn't sponsor or hold healing crusades.

They called the mission and a pastor answered the phone. *"Do you heal cats?"* they asked. The pastor said, *"Well they are God's creatures so bring it along and I'll pray for it."* They wrapped the cat in a blanket and rushed over there. The pastor prayed and the cat suddenly stood up, stretched itself, and jumped down off of the table, completely healed. The pastor took advantage of the situation and led them both to the Lord.

One time we were having a meeting on the street in our local town when a young Italian priest came up and we started talking to him. He was really sweet and although he didn't speak much English he seemed really drawn to us. We invited him to our home meeting. He showed up and really was very hungry for the Lord. The first time he came he had his dog collar and priestly garb on. The next time he brought a bag went up into the bedroom and changed into jeans and a t-shirt. He was very handsome and some of the girls showed real interest in him until we explained, "Hands off! He is a priest! "He complained that the Monsignor that he was under in the church in Kingston wouldn't let him preach the gospel.

One time we took him to a glory meeting and it was funny to see a Catholic priest marching around banging a big tambourine and praising the Lord. Whenever Kathie would talk about drinking the new wine of the spirit, he would be searching for a wine glass for a drink. He eventually returned to Italy and wrote to us to tell us that he was now involved in a Charismatic Fellowship in the Vatican.

There was an Anglican Church in Devon where the vicar was filled with the spirit, but needed some teaching. He went around with his guitar singing and telling everyone to talk in tongues. His wife wasn't spirit filled and probably wasn't saved either. We were invited down to minister to him. He had a mixed congregation of older people which a number of them had never understood the gospel. He seemed to think that the answer to all their problems was to pray for them to receive the gift of tongues. His wife however, would counsel people with problems, by sitting them down, giving them a glass of whiskey and sympathizing with them.

We started ministering to the people about free salvation and grace. One elderly person, Lady Ram had suffered a lot of guilt and condemnation from her past and couldn't find forgiveness. Eventually as we ministered truth to her she was set free and was transformed. *"And you shall know the truth and the truth shall make your free."* (John.8:32) The pastor's wife avoided us like the plague. There were so many needs that we called Tony to come and help us.

Tony arrived with his autoharp and we held a meeting at the vicarage. Most of the congregation showed up and after we preached, ministered and prayed for the people, many of them received the joy of their salvation. Tony then played and sung a well known Cameron song, '*The Holy Ghost will set your feet a dancing'* and encouraged the people to feel free to dance before the Lord. To our amazement they got up and began to take partners and waltz around the room. Just at that moment the church treasurer who hated us was passing by and heard the sound of the music and crept up and peeped through the window.

The next day she spread the rumor to the rest of the church parishioners that we were all having an orgy at the vicarage the evening before. We shook our heads and said we never knew that a bunch of old people waltzing around a room was an orgy. When we finally left we had to tell the vicar that he still had many problems to deal with including his treasurer and his wife who wasn't saved.

The vicar of St. Steven's church in East Twickenham, a town close to us, asked if we could host an African brother from Kenya by the name of Edwin Osera. Edwin was a sweet young man and stayed with us for several days and ministered at some of our meetings. We also had the opportunity to expose him to *'body ministry.'* After he returned to Kenya he invited Kathie and I to come and minister. He lived near a town called Bungoma, about 100 miles from Nairobi the capital.

Previously Kathie had been convicted because she wanted to be able to praise God in every situation. In a meeting she asked one of the brothers Barry to pray for her. Barry prayed and asked God that she would be thankful in every situation even if she found herself in a mud hut in Africa. She fell about laughing and so did everyone else, because it was ludicrous to imagine Kathie being in a mud hut in Africa. At that time we had no thoughts or way of going to Africa and Kathie was certainly not interested in going. When the invitation came, Maureen one of the ex-missionary ladies came to our house with an envelope and said, *"This is for your fare to Africa."*

Later Kathie called her and said, *"I don't really feel happy about taking this money for Africa because we have some bills to pay."*

Maureen answered, *"Well I gave it the Lord so feel free to do with it whatever you feel."*

Kathie was relieved but then Doreen another ex-missionary came with an envelope and said this is your fare for Africa. So now we were stumped. We had to go on this seven week mission trip.

Chapter Twelve
Traveling Overseas

When we arrived in Nairobi Edwin wasn't there to meet us. He came three hours later and said that he had in his mind that we were arriving tomorrow, but suddenly the Lord prompted him to come to the airport in case we already had arrived. We rented a VW Beetle for six weeks and spent the night at a nasty African hotel as Edwin said he felt uncomfortable staying at a white man's hotel. On reflection, he probably wouldn't have been allowed to stay there back then.

The next morning we left and drove for many hours out of Nairobi past the shanty town where the houses were made of cardboard, mainly on dirt roads across the rift valley, pass the soda Lake Nakuru, where thousands of Flamingoes and Pelicans feed; across to the equator at 9,000 ft. and finally down to Bungoma and on to a village called Kandui and then to a 'Shamba' which is an African farm. Edwin had built a mud hut for us to stay in and paid the expense of buying us a proper bed to sleep in. Unfortunately for me it was a single bed, so I ended up sleeping on some cushions on the baked cow dung floor.

Kathie had brought one dress and six pairs of slacks with

her. Then we found out that she couldn't wear slacks as the local Christians said that only prostitutes wore slacks, so she had to wash her one dress out everyday for seven weeks as there was no place near to buy a couple more dresses.

By this time Kathie was having a hard time and began to complain to the Lord. Fleas were biting us, the dirt walls had insects and scorpions crawling in them, the roof had rats, there was no ceiling. The chicken was as tough as leather and the breakfast oatmeal you could cut with a knife. The tea was made in a big pot full of milk and sugar then boiled all up together. It tasted very sweet, much too milky, and full of skin from the cooked milk.

One day we found an egg on our bed. Edwin said it could be the local witch doctor trying to put a spell on us or a hen jumped through the glassless window opening and laid the egg. We decided it was the hen. Edwin and Martha's little three year old daughter avoided us like the plague. She had never seen a white person before and thought we were a couple of wild animals that might eat her. In fact after a day or so she went and moved over to her grandma's Shamba and stayed there until we left.

Kathie was still complaining and fussing and suddenly she started to get this pain in her thigh. It was like a hand that kept grabbing her thigh. Every time she complained it happened. She was trying to get healed and began rebuking it. After a meeting she went out and asked God if this was some kind of African demon that was attacking her. The Lord said no it was an angel and it would continue until she started praising Him in her circumstances. So she started to thank the Lord and the pain left. As soon as she forgot and started to complain again it returned. She would get a negative attitude and it would start she would cry out, 'sorry Lord' and it would go away.

This is an excerpt from Kathie's booklet *'Angels - Watching Over You'* on page eleven. *"I remembered that I was supposed to praise the Lord all the time. I tried! I walked around gritting my teeth saying, "Praise God, Hallelujah, thank you Jesus." Inside I was fighting like a crazed gorilla! The people took us to other places to preach and each place was worse than before. I was determined that I was going to praise, so I did with clenched teeth."*

(For the complete story of Kathie's battle with the angel, which she thought was a demon, can be found in her booklet.) After struggling with her situation God finally brought healing to her, not only on her thigh, but with several other areas as well.

At one period, Edwin and his wife had to leave for three days, so we were on our own. We ran out of money and had no food. We had sent a telegram to the fellowship to send some more funds. The grandmother came over and gave us a dish of boiled green bananas. She didn't speak English so we shook her hand and nodded in thanks. I can't remember if we ate them or not, but the next day we went to the little store in Bungoma or Kandui that was owned by an Indian and picked up our funds and bought some bread, milk, cereal, cookies, candy and soda.

I was doing open air meetings in the village market place. One time I was preaching when a man came running up to me with a big stick in his hand. He rose up to strike me, but fell at my feet. It was as though he hit an invisible wall. Smack and down he went on the ground. When he finally got up, he was saved. God moved supernaturally. He then followed me on his bicycle everywhere I went to preach. He previously had the reputation of being the worst man in the village. After we left, Edwin wrote and told us that he had become one of the leading evangelists in the area.

After several open air gospel meetings the Lord asked me what I was doing. When I answered that I was faithfully preaching the Gospel, He explained to me that they had lots of visitors doing that and many of the natives were quite capable of doing it themselves. The Lord then showed me that the greatest need was to break off the poverty spirit that was rampant amongst the people. I started by telling the local preachers that they needed to work like Paul who was a tent maker. Traditionally they had been taught that if they were called to the ministry it was not only beneath them to work, but also degrading as they have been elevated to a higher level. Also the culture was such that not only the women sat separately from the men, but also walked behind them.

When a preacher went on a preaching trip he would just leave without informing or providing for his wife, and when he returned he would say nothing to her unless he was inclined to do so. I did some serious teaching on husbands love your wives as Christ loved the church. I told them to go over to their wives and show it in the meeting. I was hoping for them to go over and hug their wives and tell them how much they loved and appreciated them, but the best I got was they went across to where their wives sat and gave them a hand shake.

I explained that English culture and African culture must give precedence to scriptural teaching. The women always worked the land not the men. I told them not to just plant millet which was their main diet and sunflower seeds which they feed the pigs with. I told them to start eating the sunflower seeds themselves, (as they were healthy) and plant vegetables such as carrots, cauliflower, cabbage, beets, etc for a healthy diet and take the excess and sell them in the market place. Their lands were wonderfully fertile.

I told one man to cut the rubber off of the old scrap car and bicycle tires and make sandals and sell them. Later I was told he was becoming quite prosperous with his shoe business. My desire was that the African Christians should break away from the mentality of always looking for white folks to give them money, and become more independent and prosperous themselves.

Half way through the trip we decided to take a few days break and try to find some civilization. We drove back to Nairobi and as we entered the city we saw a Kentucky Fried Chicken. So with our tongues hanging out we staggered into heaven.

On our return to Kandui we stopped off at the rift valley and stayed with John, an English tea planter and his family at Lake Nakuru. Apart from having brown water to bath in it was great to be in some kind of comfort. We had four meals a day. The bell would ring for breakfast and we would have our granola with fresh cream from the cows which they owned. The bell would ring for lunch, then again for afternoon tea and finally at 6.00 pm for dinner. John had five children and we went on a picnic and we sat with our backs against a tree so that a lion wouldn't be able to sneak up on us. We saw thousands of the Flamingoes and Pelicans at the lake which was very smelly.

John said that his first wife who gave him all their children was not spiritual enough for him, so he prayed for the Lord to take her home. A few weeks later she suddenly died. He was now married to a missionary girl. The children we sent to England for schooling and came home for the holidays. So as it was close to Christmas they were home. I said to Kathie we had better not upset him. He might pray for the Lord to take us home early.

Just before returning home for Christmas we were invited to speak at a camp which Edwin had arranged. When we arrived our sleeping accommodation was in a cowshed along with about twelve African families. We had hammock beds to sleep on and mine broke in the middle of the night. Because there was no bathroom, only a shack with a hole in the ground about a hundred yards outside Kathie always wanted to go in the middle of the night. So I had to take her out with a flashlight and wait for her because she wasn't going on her own.

When we finally arrived home she never needed to get up in the middle of the night to use the bathroom so we decided it was psychological. We were up at 6.00 am for a cup of hot tea. No food. The meetings started at 7.00 am. - 2.00 pm. At 3.00 pm we ate. The next meeting started at 5.00 pm. – 11.00 pm. No supper. This went on for several days even through Christmas. We heard about six or eight sermons by different people in every meeting. Lots of sermons and singing were relayed through loud speakers hanging outside the large mud meeting hut.

We left after three days with a live chicken as a love gift which we gave for Edwin. We drove back to Nairobi to catch our plane back to the US.

When we arrived home, we immediately had a great feeling of appreciation to be able to sit in an easy chair, turn on the light and plug in the electric kettle to make a cup of tea. Before we left I believed that God would bless us financially and meet our needs even though we were ministering amongst the poor natives in Africa. I was disappointed that we didn't arrive back with any finances, but a few days later a large check came in the mail from Africa to bless us and our ministry from the tea planter John.

Before our trip to Kenya I had traveled to the States for the first time. Art Katz a Jewish intellectual was converted to Christianity after reading the account of the woman taken in adultery in John's Gospel. I met him when he was giving his testimony at a crusade in London hosted by an American evangelist. I invited him and his Jewish Christian friend Paul Gordon to our Sunday meeting and had the opportunity to introduce both of them to New Testament body ministry. They came and stayed with us for a few days and were completely captivated by the freedom of our meetings.

Others were coming from the States to visit us to see what God was doing. A prophet, Gordon Devorés, came with his pastor, Willard Jarvis, from Columbus, Ohio to visit. They had been to Chard and were now visiting us. They were really blessed with the meetings and had the opportunity to share. They invited me to come and minister at their church. When Paul and Art found out I was coming to the US they asked me to visit them. When I arrived in New York, Art Katz met me. I spent several days with Paul and a short time with Art. I ministered in New Jersey and North Carolina before going to Ohio to speak at a youth camp hosted by Pastor Willard Jarvis' church.

Kathie and I began to receive more invitations to come to minister in the US. On one of the early visits we sold our car to cover the air fares. I advertised the car and eventually a dealer came and made me a fair offer for the car. I sold him the car, but about two weeks later he called saying he wanted to see me about the car. At first my heart sank as I thought he was going to ask for his money back because he found something wrong with the car. He finally arrived at our house and said that he had sold the car, but he felt he should give me more money for it. And then he handed me a bunch of notes that when totaled with what he had previously paid me, more than covered our air fares. In the natural, dealers just don't do things like that, but we were moving in the supernatural.

After our trip to Kenya we were both invited back to the States to minister. One of those times we ministered at a family camp hosted by Pastor Willard's church. They had three speakers, one for the adults, one for the teens and one for the children. I was scheduled to minister to the teens. They were somewhat hardened and we were waiting for a breakthrough. One afternoon before the evening service at the chapel I felt I should minister to the children. I asked if I could and we went with about 25 of them into a prefab building. As I ministered the Holy Spirit fell and the children went under a very strong anointing. Many of them began to have prophetic visions. Others were crying, shaking and praying with great intensity. As we were nearing the end of the meeting, the chapel bell began to ring for evening service. The chapel was up on the hill which was quite a distance from where we were situated.

The children flocked out of the building and made their way up to the chapel still with the anointing all over them. We got in our car and began to drive up the hill to the chapel and by this time the children had caught up with the teenagers who were dragging their feet. As we drove by we suddenly saw the teenagers fall out on the grass as the children came amongst them. All kinds of manifestations started taking place and the teens were drunk with the spirit and were half being carried along.

When we arrived in the chapel Erskine Holt the speaker for the evening was checking his notes, and the worship team were tuning up their instruments. Suddenly the doors burst open and in came the children and teens and as they did, the power of God fell on everyone. Somebody screamed out I'm healed. Gifts began to flow, miracles began to happen and people's lives were transformed. Brother Erskine wisely put aside his notes for his sermon and just let God take over. The next night the same thing happened again and God just came down in a tangible way and dwelt amongst us. Everyone was ministered to and nobody preached.

One time when I was preaching at Pastor Willard Jarvis' church in Columbus Ohio, I called the young people up to the platform to be prayed for. I then sat down in a pew next to Pastor Willard and waited. The teens were giggling and feeling stupid standing there. It was about twenty minutes later when suddenly the Spirit of God hit them and they were soon shaking, crying, and falling down. Revival broke out on those youngsters.

Pastor Willard said to me that if it had been him he would have closed the meeting after about five minutes as nothing was happening. He said, *"I guess I need to learn to trust the Holy Spirit more."* Some time later I wrote a book called *'Kids in Combat.'* I included that incident in the book. Some years later, I received a letter from a youth pastor who said she had read the book and that particular incident. Sometime later she was having a meeting with the youth and they prayed for each other then began giggling and acting silly. She remembered the story in the book and sat down and waited and within about ten minutes the same thing happened as the Holy Spirit came down on the youth and revival broke out. During the many times Kathie and I returned to Pastor Willard's church we had great moves of the spirit.

Chapter Thirteen

Dealing with Demons & Spirit led Evangelism

One time a few of the missionary girls from our fellowship were having some demonic activity at their rented house which they had just moved into. Things were moving around like the furniture and utensils. They asked Kathie if she would go over to their house and pray.

When she arrived they said the activity was mostly on the upper level. As she climbed the stairs something punched her arm then she went into one room where the closet doors were opening and shutting and plates and pictures were flying around the room. In another bedroom similar things were happening. Back down in the hallway she noticed a trunk that belonged to the person who owned the house and she had left it there. Kathie opened the trunk and found books and objects of a strange religion. Kathie told all the spirits to leave and they took the trunk outside and put it in the garage. After that there were no more problems in the house.

In Leicester we were taken by Steve and his wife Di' (who had recently been filled with the spirit after visiting our fellowship) to visit Wendy who was hungry; even desperate to experience the fullness of the Spirit. Her husband Eric, who was a very religious evangelical and a lay preacher had heard about us, but avoided us like the plague.

After we ministered to Wendy we were having a cup of tea when he came in from work, when he saw us and found out who we were he nearly died. But then when he saw what had happened to Wendy he was impressed, so his fears and objections began to disappear. He started to listen intently to what we had to say. After spending time with him we found out that he was addicted to railway time tables and had drawers and boxes full of them.

He eventually was delivered from them and some religious strongholds, and was filled with the spirit and became a pastor of a church near in a town called Reading. We kept in contact with Eric and Wendy and they visited our fellowship several times before he became a pastor. They even visited us after we moved to America, as did Steve and Di.

There was an interesting situation that happened at our Sunday morning meeting one time. Renowned healing evangelist Morris Cerullo was preaching at the Royal Albert hall in London. During his meetings a little old lady would go up into the balcony and suddenly scream out in tongues and wouldn't stop. Cerullo had to have her removed, but she would creep back into the next service and do it again. Haydn, one of our young people, who didn't know who she was, saw her at the Saturday service just as everyone was leaving and enthusiastically invited her to come to our Sunday morning meeting. Unfortunately I didn't know that he had done this.

The next Sunday morning at the meeting I noticed a little white haired old lady appeared at the entrance of the meeting hall. She was a little late and the place was packed. One of our elders sitting on the front saw her, smiled and called out, *"Welcome Sister! There is room down here at the front, come and take a seat."* She mumbled something regarding her testimony and made her way down to the front row.

As soon as I saw her my heart sank as I knew who she was. I thought if Morris Cerullo wasn't able to deal with or deliver her, who were we? It wasn't long before she began to scream out in tongues. Barry one of the mature brothers moved across and put his hand on her shoulder trying to quiet her down, but she continued. I came up from where I was sitting and said, *"Sister, please stop and be quiet."*

She opened one eye, glared up at me and said, *"Don't quench the Holy Spirit brother!"*

I replied, *"I know you! You're the one that tried to wreck the Morris Cerullo meetings. You are out of here."*

I grabbed her and with the help of two brothers began to escort her out. It wasn't easy as she was hitting me with her umbrella and screaming, *"Don't touch God's anointed."*

Some of the new visitors thought I was being mean to her as she looked like such a sweet, little, old, harmless, lady, with her pretty hat on her white haired head, but she was full of religious demons. We were on the second floor so we had to half carry her down which wasn't easy as she was quiet portly and she was still trying to hit us with her umbrella and her big wicker shopping basket. When we finally got her out she looked up at our building and said, *"This isn't even a proper church, it looks more like a town hall to me,"* and she went stomping off.

Even though we were upset about her coming, it was funny and we need to have a sense of humor and not take ourselves too seriously, especially when embarrassing things happen.

Another strange thing we had to deal with was when two older women arrived at our house meeting. As it was crowded they sat on the stairs. During the meetings they suddenly began making loud wailing noises like cats. Tao, our Siamese cat began to join in. I asked them what they were doing and they said, *"We are making intercession with groanings which cannot be uttered."* (Rom. 8:26).

There was also another large older eastern European woman present who was blocking the stairs, so people couldn't get by to use the bathroom. We asked her to move, but she refused. We tried several times to persuade her, but she remained firm saying she was crippled and needed prayer. We eventually got her to move with prayer and assistance. Fortunately neither of those ladies showed up again.

When you have revival you have to deal with messes. If

you are frightened of a mess then don't even think about a revival. *"Where no oxen are, the trough is clean; but much increase comes by the strength of an ox."* (Prov.14:4) Many churches are so concerned about being clean and sterile that they lack spiritual life; or any life for that matter.

In the old realm people would go out on the streets and witness to people or they would have thousands of tracts printed and either mail them out or go from door to door with them like the Jehovah Witnesses. It was the numbers game. If you talk to as many people as you can you must win a few by the law of averages. After we were filled with the Spirit that concept didn't seem right for us. We didn't want a hit and miss ministry, we wanted to see God's hand it everything we did.

Harry Greenwood encouraged us when we heard how the Lord used him to bring a whole neighborhood into revival. He was driving along and the Lord told him to turn right and then left, then to drive down a street and stop at a certain house number. He obeyed and the Lord told him there was a sick boy there and to knock on the door and pray for him and the Lord would heal him.

He knocked and a women opened the door, *"You have a sick boy!"* said Harry.

"Yes. Come in," replied the women.

Apparently she thought he was the doctor. Harry went upstairs to the bedroom and ministered and prayed for the boy and he was instantly healed and got out of bed. Then things began to happen and the mother and her husband accepted the Lord and were filled with the spirit. They then asked Harry to come back and have a meeting and they would invite their neighbors.

Within a few days the whole street was saved. Ian Andrews then followed it up with more miracles, healings, salvations and the baptism of the Spirit. How much better it is to be led by the Spirit rather than use human resources to minister the gospel.

I remember Bible teacher Bob Mumford telling an amusing story after Harry had ministered in his area.

He said, *"Harry so raised my faith that I felt I could believe for anything."*

So when he heard Harry tell that story, he said, *"I will try this,"* so he got in his car and started to drive.

He felt led to turn at the next corner. Then these words came to him, *"Drive 100 yards, turn right, then go down to the end and you will see a small dirt road, turn there and go to the third house on the left where there is a sick person."*

He was so excited; as he turned down the dirt road, everything was accurate so far, but as he drove down, it wasn't just that there was no third house there weren't any houses at all.

That reminded me of Frank. I don't know if Bob Mumford gave up on being led like that, or he persevered. If at first you don't succeed (quit) or try, try, again?

Arthur Burt would tell how Harry believed in prosperity

when he lived in a caravan and had stinging-nettle soup for food and when he preached was given only fifty shillings just enough to get him gas for his old junky car to travel to the next meeting. After persevering with his revelation, he ended up buying the mayor's house with a swimming pool and owing a Jaguar to prove how his faith worked for him.

When Harry stayed with us one time and it was Kathie's birthday.

She said to the Lord, *"I would like some perfume called, 'Joy', but is it too expensive?"*

Harry was over at Timmy's house teaching at a Bible study. When Kathie went over there to the Bible study, Harry suddenly looked up and said, *"You shall have 'Joy' always."*

After the Bible study finished Kathie made lunch for Harry before he left. On his way out he said, *"I put some cold cash in the refrigerator."* It was 30 pounds sterling which was exactly the amount for the perfume.

After traveling to the US on several occasions we finally moved here in 1978. South African preacher, Robert Thom, (who wrote the popular book "The New Wine is Better") was ministering at one of our friend's fellowships. We attended the meeting and he had a word for us that God was going to take us out of the nest. This was the final conformation for our move.

After experiencing the ministry of a pasturing a local church in the US we eventually worked with a campus ministry and then became international; working with children, youth and parents. Many thousands of children, parents and teens and hundreds of churches were affected by the spirit of revival. Hundreds of youth and children's pastors were touched and senior pastors changed their whole outlook on young people as God moved in a mighty way amongst them with miracles, signs and wonders. Also revival broke out in schools and juvenile detention centers.

A Testimony received on Dec 21st 2010.

Hi Dave and Kathie,

In the early 70's you both came to my school (GILLINGHAM, Kent, England) with Stuart. You sang a song called, "You gotta be a Baby to come to Jesus," in our school assembly. I had never met anyone before who had no thought for their own reputation and a total disregard to for what others thought of them. I immediately knew that you had something that I did not have and that I must have it at all costs. I gave my life to the Lord in the follow up meeting. I attended Hempstead Christian fellowship, (as it then was) and for the next 35 years. I am still going strong in the Lord. Praise God! Praise His Anointing! I have been aware that those who have enjoyed the manifest presence of God over the years, have been those with a David heart - that have sought the purposes of God, having a total disregard to for what others thought of them. God is the same yesterday, today and forever! I heard your name mentioned on a

CD today and looked you up. I hope that this email brings you encouragement and demonstrates that what you have done over the years has a lasting value.

God bless – Terry.

CONCLUSION

"Although the events are historically correct, due to the long term time lapse from the 1970's to 2012, we cannot guarantee that every event is in chronological order."

David and Kathie Walters

There are many good things happening in the church today, but there still is a lot of religion and control. Some of the mega-churches and mega-ministries are having a positive impact on many people. With the gifted ministries, huge finances and faithful supporters they have accomplished a great amount. Even with the critics who accuse some of them (with possible justification) of living opulent lifestyles.

In Britain the religious mentality was (and to some extent still exists) is to keep preachers poor, to keep them humble. The poverty spirit is still strong in many areas of the religious realm and many church people don't seriously support the work of the Lord.

When we get old there is a danger of harping after the good old days and saying things were better than they are now. People who are now in their twenty through forties will probably say the same thing when they get to their sixties through eighties. So is '*body ministry*' the simple organic and spontaneous meeting no longer relevant for the church today? With all of our Hi-tech equipment and professional music, our Bible teachers, seminary graduates and Doctors of theology and beautiful buildings, have we passed and are better equipped than the primitive church?

Many of the academic and reformed preachers strain at perfecting their sermons, rather than perfecting the saints. Was true Christianity supposed to be an evolution? The Spirit of God is still moving even though many are still stuck in the historic events, be they pre-reformation or post-reformation and still preach in Elizabethan English. The question is do we hold onto religious traditions more than the teaching and spirit of the scriptures?

As previously mentioned the tradition of the evangelical church (because it had no ritual as the older historic churches practiced) had what was known as the 'hymn sandwich,' which was an opening hymn, a reading, another hymn, the notices, the offering, another hymn, the message, a final hymn, then the benediction. In the charismatic churches we start with a period of worship (with the worship team) then the notices, the message and then ministry; which more often than not doesn't connect.

As explained earlier, it's like having a meal where you eat everything separately. If my grandson has a meal of meat, peas and potatoes, he eats the peas first, then the potatoes, and lastly the meat. This seems very strange and monotonous to most people who like to mix their food and eat some of each to make the meal more enjoyable. What true in the natural is also true in the spiritual and that's why so many people find church boring, because it's predictable and much of the same old, same old; especially if they have previously been in meetings where everything is spirit led and spontaneous; so that worship is intermingled with prophecies, revelations, teaching, giving, and testimonies.

When Jesus spoke to Nicodemas and told him be must be born again; He went on to reveal that those that are born of the spirit are like the wind. It blows where it wishes, you hear the sound of it, but you don't know where is coming from or where it's going. (See John 3:8) So if we born again Christians are to be like the wind, unpredictable, (not unreliable) then surely when we gather together corporately, should not our meetings also be unpredictable? In other words, we come and gather together with the excitement and expectancy of God's Spirit showing up and taking over. How about a church meeting of "Suddenly's" next Sunday morning?

Most Charismatic churches has its own flavor and as the worship is set by the worship leader it doesn't necessarily connect to the message or the ministry so the members of the congregation play no or very little part in the service. The more professional we become the better the service is, but then we usually end up having a good service, rather than a God meeting.

The new wine is still being poured out (we see it all the time in our meetings) but in many cases the wineskin doesn't change so the basic man-made religious format is still maintained. It modernizes a little, but it's still the same old wineskin.

Praise God! There are remnants of saints who still hunger and cry after the wonderful, exciting, powerful, spontaneous, organic church where the Holy Spirit has complete control and revival prevails. "Oh Yes" it's not perfect; sometimes silly funny and crazy things happen, but that's life. We can deal with the messes by allowing people to make them, we learn by our mistakes. No one person gets the credit or glory as God continues to use all and sundry. Literally hundreds of people want this, but can't find it and are forced to put up with something less.

This book is not about mainstream Christianity; it doesn't appeal to the majority of churchgoers or those that worship, applaud, and follow their spiritual heroes without question. But if you are one of the hungry ones who desire the simple presence and working of the Holy Spirit then go for it.

If you can't find a church or anyone where this is happening or accepted where you live, find some hungry ones and gather together with them and learn to rely on the Holy Spirit to open your eyes and guide you. Search for others and bring unbelievers into a spiritual realm where they will learn to live and walk in the supernatural by faith. *"But the anointing which you have received from Him abides in you, and you do no need anyone to teach you; but as the same anointing teaches you concerning all things, which is true, and not a lie, and just as it has taught you, you will abide in Him."* (1.John.2:27)

Although David and Kathie Walters are now in their seventies they are still very active in ministry. David teaches and ministers both nationally and internationally. His *'Holy Spirit Encounters'* for families brings everyone into the anointing. Kathie holds numerous meetings in the US and in many countries abroad, teaching and prophetically ministering to people on how to come into all that God has for you. She declares that, "Normal Christianity offers to believers, an experience of the realm of the spirit, which includes the supernatural, angels, heavenly visitations, and miracles, which are all part of our inheritance. If we don't have them, then we are being ripped off by religious devils." Kathie also takes groups on her Celtic Tours to Scotland and Ireland. Both David and Kathie have spoken at numerous Christian conferences and appeared many times on National and local Christian TV & Radio; including TBN with Mark Chironna - Day-Star - It's Supernatural with Sid Roth. They have authored 28 books between them.

For information on their bio's, itineraries, articles, books, e-books CD's and DVD's go to www.kathiewaltersministry.com or www.goodnews.netministries.org Also call Good News Ministries at 478-757-8071 For orders 800-300-9630.

Other Books by David and Kathie Walters

The Bright and Shining Revival - An account of the Hebrides Revival 1948 – 1952. The praying men and women of the Hebrides clung to the promise that if they sought Him, He would HEAL THEIR LAND. Read what happened when the power of God descended on the communities of these Scottish Islands."

Angels Watching over You - Did you know that Angels are very active in our everyday lives?

Celtic Flames -Discover the exciting accounts of famous Fourth & Fifth Century Celtic Christians: Patrick, Brendan, Cuthbert, Brigid and others.

Columba - The Celtic Dove - Read about the prophetic and miraculous ministry of this famous Celtic Christian, filled with supernatural visitations.

Living in the Supernatural - Kathie believes that the supernatural realm, the angels, miracles, and signs and wonders are the spiritual inheritance of every believer, as in the early church

For further information or order forms
please call or write:

Good News Fellowship Ministries
220 Sleepy Creek Rd. Macon Georgia 31210

Phone (478) 757-8071 fax (478) 757-0136
E-mail: goodnews@reynoldscable.net
http://www.goodnews.netministries.org.

Made in the USA
Charleston, SC
01 November 2012